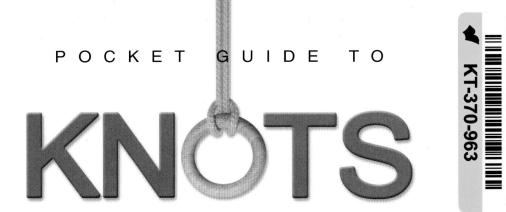

POCKET GUIDE TO
KNOTS

POCKET GUIDE TO

KNOTS

Maria Costantino

Published by SILVERDALE BOOKS
An imprint of Bookmart Ltd
Registered number 2372865
Trading as Bookmart Ltd
Blaby Road
Wigston
Leicester LE18 4SE

© 2006 D&S Books Ltd

D&S Books Ltd
Kerswell,
Parkham Ash, Bideford
Devon, England
EX39 5PR

e-mail us at:- enquiries@d-sbooks.co.uk

This edition printed 2006

ISBN 1-84509-290-2

DS0101. Pocket Knots

Creative Director: Sarah King
Designer: Debbie Fisher
Photographer: Paul Forrester

The material in this book is revised and
previously appeared in The Knot Handbook

Font: Helvetica

Printed in Thailand

1 3 5 7 9 10 8 6 4 2

Contents

Introduction

Most of us use the word 'knot' to mean that frustrating tangle in a piece of string, cord, or even in our shoelaces. Strictly speaking, however, a knot is a connection in a cord or length of rope that has been formed in one of two ways. Firstly, by passing one free end of a piece of rope through a loop and drawing it tight. Secondly, a knot can be made by intertwining or tying together two pieces of rope or cord.

There are, however, a number of very different groups of knot, and each knot serves a different purpose. Stopper knots prevent the ends of a rope from fraying and also stop the rope from being pulled through a pulley block or any other opening. Stopper knots are also used to weight the end of a length of rope to make it easier to throw. Shortening knots are used to form nooses and loops and to shorten a length of rope instead of cutting the rope with a blade. Binding knots serve two purposes: they can confine and constrict a single object or length of rope or they can be used to hold closely together two or more objects or lengths of ropes. Hitches are used to tie a rope around an object like a pole, spar or ring, while a bend is a knot that ties two ropes together.

It is estimated that some 90 per cent of all recorded knots were devised by sailors, while the remaining 10 per cent came from occupations as diverse as anglers and archers, bookmakers and butchers, carpenters and climbers, surgeons

and stevedores, and, of course, from the executioner, who gave us the hangman's knot! Clifford W. Ashley (1881–1947), who was born in the whaling port of New Bedford, Massachusetts, was one of the world's leading authorities on knots and knot-tying. His book, The Ashley Book of Knots, first published in 1944, has become the bible of dedicated knot-tyers. In it, Ashley describes nearly 4,000 knots, with 7,000 drawings.

None of these professions can truly be said to be the originators of knots, since the first people to tie knots were likely to have been the cave-dwellers who learned to hunt and fish and needed knots for their bows and arrows, traps, fishing nets and lines. Archaeological evidence some 10,000 years old shows that Neolithic man used overhand knots, half-hitches, clove hitches, reef knots and nooses.

Throughout history, and across the world, knots and knotted cords have been important: they have been used as calendars and records of important events, as tallies to record trading transactions and as mnemonic devices to cue the memory. It is likely that the abacus, the forerunner of today's calculators, and the rosary that is used to count off prayers, were both devised from simple knotted cords.

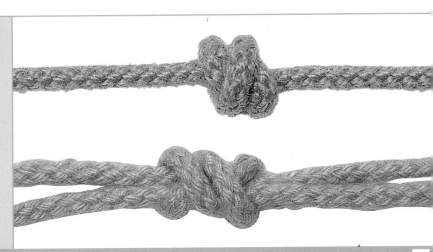

A classic example of a stopper knot – the double overhand knot.

The surgeon's knot is a useful binding knot.

Knots also feature in mythology. The most famous mythological knot is the Gordian Knot. The legend goes that Gordius, a simple peasant, rose to become the king of Phrygia. As ruler, he no longer needed his farm cart, so he tied the harness traces into an intricate knot and presented it as an offering to the god Zeus in his temple. No one seemed able to untie the knot and the oracle of the temple prophesied that whoever undid the Gordian Knot was destined to be the ruler of all Asia. When Alexander the Great saw the knotty problem before him, he wasted no time: he severed the knot with his sword. Technically, the knot was undone and the prophecy was fulfilled, and consequently today 'cutting the Gordian Knot' means to act quickly and decisively in a difficult situation.

Although each knot serves a different purpose, it really isn't necessary to know hundreds of knots. After all, Neolithic man

The Jansik special is a very strong hitch.

survived with just a handful! However, it is important to understand how different knots are best suited to the conditions in which they are to be used.

One of the main reasons for selecting one knot rather than another is the relative strength of the knot. Knot strengths are of particular importance to climbers, who will favour bulky knots with several wrapping turns. These types of knots are designed to absorb strain and to avoid weakening the rope. Climbers routinely check their knots on a climb, especially when stiff rope is used, because it is more difficult to tie, being less flexible. Consequently, climbers check regularly to make sure that their knots are secure. Other factors that influence knot choice are the speed and ease of tying, the size of knot and the reliability of the knot.

The sheet bend is unusual in that it can be tied using two different diameters of rope.

Learning the ropes

Understanding the properties of rope and knowing how to keep it in good condition are essential to the knot-tyer. The word 'rope' is generally defined as meaning any plaited, braided or laid (that is, in strands) product

The term 'rope' properly descibes a product over 10mm (5/12 inches) in diameter.

Anything smaller than 10mm (5/12 inches) is classified as cord, twine or thread. The strength of fine cord can be increased by plaiting.

over 10mm (5/12 inches) in diameter. (There are some exceptions, however, as some specialised climbing ropes are 9mm (3/8 inches) in diameter.) Anything smaller is called cord, twine, or thread.

Rope and cord are known collectively as cordage, but are also often referred to as stuff. When rope or cord is used to do a particular job, it becomes a line, such as a washing line, a tow line or a life line. Sometimes, some lines have even more specific names: a lightweight throwing or heaving line that is used to haul a heavier line across a gap – such as from the deck of a boat, across the water to the jetty - is known as a messenger.

Materials and construction

The properties of a rope are determined by the material from which it is made, as well as by the way in which the rope has been constructed.

Until the twentieth century, all rope was made of vegetable fibre, which came from a variety of sources: plants stems, such as flax and jute, leaves of agave (sisal) and abaca (hemp), fibrous coconut shells (coir), silk, wool, camel, and even human hair, have all been used.

While these natural fibres are attractive, they do have their drawbacks. When wet, natural-fibre ropes swell, and consequently any knots tied in them become impossible to untie. In icy conditions, these ropes will freeze, and the brittle fibres are damaged and broken, reducing the strength of the rope. Natural-fibre ropes are also unable to stand great amounts of abrasion, and are furthermore prone to mildew, rot and decay caused by insects and vermin.

Coir rope, made from the fibres of coconut shells is the weakest of the natural-fibre ropes, and to compensate it is made in very large sizes. It floats on water, but also stretches, and today it is rarely used outside the Pacific and India, except for boat fenders.

For centuries, hemp was the predominant rope-making material. Its historical and economic importance can still be seen today, reflected in many place names in England, such as Hemel Hempstead, once a thriving centre for the trade in hemp.

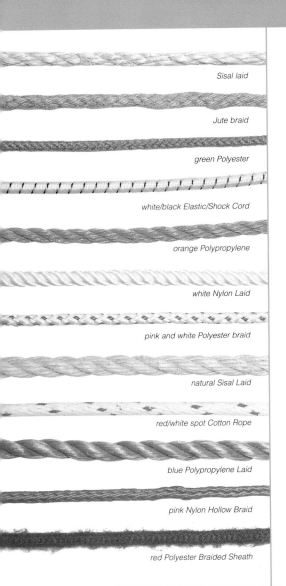

Sisal laid

Jute braid

green Polyester

white/black Elastic/Shock Cord

orange Polypropylene

white Nylon Laid

pink and white Polyester braid

natural Sisal Laid

red/white spot Cotton Rope

blue Polypropylene Laid

pink Nylon Hollow Braid

red Polyester Braided Sheath

Hemp fibres are produced from the stalk of the plant Cannabis sativa and make the strongest of all the natural-fibre ropes, although it does have a low durability as it is subject to decay.

As strong as hemp, but more durable, is Manila rope, whose fibres are obtained from the leaves of the plant Musa textilis. Manila was widely used until the Second World War, but today it is only available from specialist sources and at a premium price. A good general-purpose rope is sisal. This is an inexpensive fibre made from the leaves of the plant Agave sisalana. Pale in colour and hairy to the touch, sisal ropes can also be purchased waterproofed for use in damp or wet environments. Now mainly used for decorative rope, cotton was once one of the most popular natural-fibre ropes for making fishing nets. The smooth, soft fibres did, however, require treating to prevent rot. The cordage made from these vegetable sources is known as natural fibre, and ropes made from them are usually made as a laid rope.

Laid rope

Three-strand, or laid rope, is made of natural fibres which have been twisted together in a clockwise (or right-handed) direction to create long yarns. Several of these yarns are then twisted together in an anti-clockwise (or left-handed) direction to create a strand. Then, three strands are twisted together in a clockwise (right-handed) direction to create the typical rope known as a hawser. The direction of the twist in a three-strand rope is called the lay of the rope. Rope is described as S-laid (left-laid) or Z-laid (right laid). Most three-strand rope is Z-laid. It is unusual, but not unknown, to have S-laid rope: it is generally found in cable which is made from three lengths of Z-laid ropes twisted together.

It is the counteracting directions of the twists in a rope that give it its strength and produce enough friction to keep it in shape. Even when a strand is uncoiled from a rope, the remaining two strands will still cling together and it is possible to see the gap where the missing strand would lie. Until the Second World War, all rope was generally laid, or three-strand construction.

An Alpine coil, using a synthetic rope made in the laid manner.

Synthetic (manmade) cordage

Although natural-fibre ropes are strong, because the fibres are short and do not extend the entire length of the rope, they are not as strong as synthetic ropes, which are made from fibres that are one continuous length. A three-strand, or laid, nylon rope is more than twice as strong as a Manila rope of the same length. Furthermore, the nylon rope weighs half as much and is four times more durable.

Developed by the chemical industries in the early part of the twentieth century, a wide range of synthetic ropes has been developed since the Second World War. Synthetic-fibre cordage can comprise single, round fibres called monofilaments, clusters of round multifilaments, staples (made by cutting mono- or multifilaments into short lengths) or flat, narrow, ribbon-like fibres. All synthetic ropes share the same characteristics: they all have high tensile (breaking) strengths and load-bearing qualities; they can absorb shock; they don't rot or degrade in sea water and are generally resistant to chemical damage; and they absorb less water than natural-fibre ropes, so their breaking strains remain constant even when they are wet. Synthetic cordage can even be dyed, so cordage can be colour-coded according to its use.

While synthetic cordage is not subject to the problems that affect natural-fibre ropes, they do, nevertheless, have their own disadvantages. Synthetic ropes are more susceptible to heat generated by friction:

they can become soft, they can melt, and, in extreme circumstances, ropes can part. Furthermore, because synthetic ropes are often very smooth, knots can easily slip undone. Where natural-fibre ropes have their own 'in-built' resistance to slippage, knots tied in synthetic ropes need to be secured by an extra tuck or half-hitch. Slippage in synthetic ropes can also be overcome by constructing laid ropes.

Synthetic rope is stronger, more hard-wearing and lighter in weight than natural rope.

Polyester rope is ideal when high-tensile strength is required, such as in a rescue situation.

The most common synthetic materials are polyamide (nylon) – still one of the strongest materials used to produce rope – polyester and polypropylene, as well as the more recently developed aramid and HMP (high modulus polyethylene).

Nylon was the first synthetic material to be used for rope-making. It is very elastic

Nylon rope is preferred by climbers as it absorbs shock and stretches.

and under load can be stretched between 10 and 40 per cent and then regain its original length once the load is removed.

Consequently, nylon rope is most suitable for absorbing shock loads: climbers use it, as it can absorb the energy of a fall, and it can also be used for mooring and towing lines. Nylon rope does not float and, when wet, it can lose between 5 and 25 per cent of its strength. While nylon rope can be bought in different colours, white nylon rope is, in fact, stronger. As well as adding to the cost, colouring nylon weakens it by as much as 10 per cent.

Polyester rope has 75 per cent of the strength of nylon, but polyester ropes are equally strong, wet or dry. Like nylon, a polyester rope does not float, and much of its inherent elasticity can be removed by pre-stretching during manufacture. Consequently, polyester ropes are used when stretch is not required, but a high-tensile strength is needed.

Available in a number of forms, polypropylene ranks between

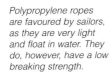

Polypropylene ropes are favoured by sailors, as they are very light and float in water. They do, however, have a low breaking strength.

natural fibres and the superior synthetics (nylon and polyester). Polypropylene fibres make inexpensive, all-purpose ropes that are light and that float. This makes them very useful for short mooring lines, rescue lines and for use in activities like water-skiing.

Polypropylene ropes, however, have only one-third of the breaking strength of nylon ropes, and, because the melting point is quite low (around 150°C/302°F), they cannot be used for any task where friction could generate that amount of heat. Furthermore, polypropylene ropes have low resistance to abrasion and must be stored out of direct sunlight, as they tend to disintegrate when exposed to UV light.

The more recently developed 'miracle' fibres are extremely strong and light. Aramid fibres such as 'Kevlar', developed by Du Pont in 1965, is twice as strong as nylon, but with a low elasticity. An extremely versatile fibre, Kevlar is most famous for being the fibre used to make bulletproof vests. In ropes, however, tight curves and knots reduce strength, so aramid fibres are used for the core of ropes, which are protected by a braided sheath made from another material. HMP, or high modulus polyethylene, is the strongest fibre developed so far. Super-lightweight, but with a tensile strength greater than stainless steel, HMP is used for the core of rope, for fishing lines and in industries where extra safety margins are required. Because they are expensive, HMP ropes are not recommended for practising knot-tying.

Knots not only have a practical use, but can be very decorative, too, as demonstrated by this jury mast knot.

Types of rope

Some synthetic ropes are made in the 'old' way, as laid rope, in order to recreate some of the particular handling qualities of the older, natural cordage. Other synthetic ropes are produced as braided (or plaited) or as sheath-and-core ropes. Braided rope can be constructed in a variety of ways but the most common forms are made up of eight or sixteen braids. Some braided cordage is hollow; this makes a very flexible rope, but it does flatten out during use. In most cases, a separate core is used to give strength and elasticity, while a braided outer sheath reinforces the whole rope. The inner core may be braided or laid, but braid-on-braid is generally considered the strongest method of cordage construction.

Climbing ropes are a special class of cordage and are often referred to as kernmantel. Kernmantels consist of a core (or kern) and a braided outer sheath (or mantel). Climbers use static ropes to take the full weight of the climber that are designed for wear-and-tear and the occasional short fall of a rock face. Dynamic ropes are safety ropes. These are not generally for carrying the climber's weight, but, because they are designed with extra elasticity and

Climbers use special 'sheath-and-core' ropes, designed with extra elasticity and strength.

strength, dynamic ropes are used in case of particularly dangerous falls and the uncontrolled spinning of a climber who has fallen.

Due to the heat generated by friction during rappelling (abseiling) and belaying, climbing ropes need high melting points. Obtain specialist advice on the different properties of climbing ropes from climbing associations and specialist suppliers, and look for the label of approval from the UIAA (Union Internationale des Associations d'Alpinisme).

Rope-makers' product information will give specification tables listing average breaking loads for each type and size of cordage. If you intend to climb, pothole, sail, dive or glide – in short, take part in any activity where your life may depend on the properties of the rope that you use – you will need to 'learn the ropes'! For knot-tyers, a more generalised knowledge that will help you to select your rope on the basis of function, appearance and price is all that is needed.

A nylon braid over an inner core provides both strength and elasticity.

Rope Maintenance

Looking after ropes makes perfect sense, as rope in good condition can be relied on to do its job safely and effectively. Well-maintained rope will also last longer and make knot-tying easier. Here are some tips for looking after your ropes.

- Untie knots as soon as possible after use – leaving knots in place will weaken ropes.

- Do not leave rope (or even smaller stuff, like cotton or string) exposed to bright sunlight. Remember that some polypropylene ropes degrade in UV light.

- Avoid contamination from acids, alkalis, oils and organic solvents.

- Protect synthetic cordage from heat and sparks.

- Wash sand, grit and oil off ropes in warm water containing household washing-up liquid.

- For ropes that have been in sea water, at the end of the season, before they are put away in storage, soak and rinse ropes in fresh water to remove salt deposits.

- Make sure that all ropes – synthetic and natural fibre – are thoroughly dry before storing them away.

- Store cordage in a cool, dry, dark place, with good air circulation.

- Inspect your ropes periodically. Go over them yard by yard and look for worn or broken surfaces.

- Do not walk on ropes.

- Coil ropes loosely and hang them on pegs well above the floor.

- Never leave rope lying loose on the floor. It could become damaged and cause accidents.

Cordage Care

Whether you are uncoiling a new length of rope for the first time or storing an old rope, it is important to know how to coil and uncoil rope correctly. Not only is coiled rope aesthetically pleasing, but coiling will help to prevent the rope from fraying and acquiring kinks – deformations in the rope caused by too tight loops which can damage and weaken the rope.

Chapter 1 gives examples of various coiling techniques. It also includes some examples of whipping rope to prevent the ends fraying. Whipping provides an attractive finish to a rope, although it can be time-consuming.

An alternative to whipping – although not as attractive – is to use adhesive tape. Tape can also be helpful when cutting rope.

Try to avoid using broad, sawing motions when cutting. This will minimise the fray and stop the tape from sliding around the rope.

Other methods of securing the ends of rope include a propriety whipping liquid; dipping the ends of small-diameter rope or thin lines into a latex-based glue; and specialised plastic tubing fitted over the ends of rope. The plastic shrinks into a tight seal when the ends are held over the steam of a boiling kettle.

Cutting Cord

1 Wrap two turns of tape around the rope or cord where the cut is to be made.

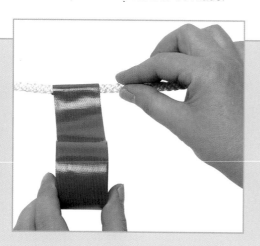

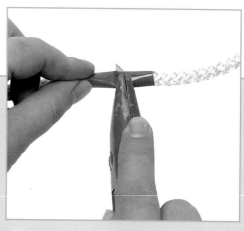

2 Using a sharp blade, cut vertically down through the middle of the taped portion.

If rope ends are not sealed, the ends will fray and become unworkable.

Get knotted!

Apart from a length of rope, the only requirements that you will need for tying the knots illustrated in this book are practice and an understanding of the terms used to describe the different parts of a rope and the ways in which the rope is figured.

Terms

Anyone who ties a knot is known as a tyer, and not a tier. This is because when it is written, the word tyer cannot also mean a row of seats in a theatre or a layer of a wedding cake.

Parts of a rope

The end of a rope that is actively involved in the knot-tying process is known as the working end. (Anglers may, however, also call it the tag end.)

The remaining part of the rope is called the standing part. At the end of the standing part of the rope – that is, the other end, away from the end you are working with – is the standing end. This standing end just 'sits' there, hopefully being very well behaved!

Tip: To help you remember which end of your rope is the working end, colour-code your whipping. You could use some coloured adhesive tape for this.

The parts of a rope

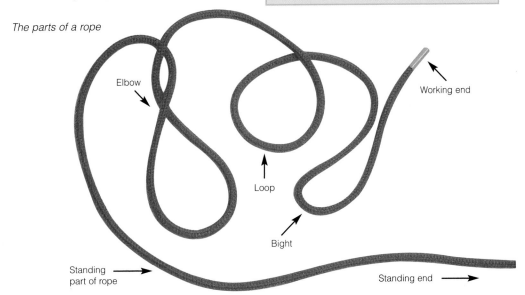

Elbow

Working end

Loop

Bight

Standing part of rope

Standing end

Rope that is folded back on itself without crossing over creates a bight. You can create a bight to locate the exact centre of a piece of rope: when you have done this you have middled the rope.

When the two adjacent parts of a rope cross over, a bight turns into a loop. A simple loop is an overhand loop. This is when the working end of the rope lies on top of the standing part. (An underhand loop is reversed: the working end lies underneath the standing part.) Add an extra twist to the loop and you will create an elbow.

Turns

A turn is when a rope passes around one side of an object or rope. A round turn is when the rope completes one-and-a-half circles around an object or a rope. Crossing turns are the basis of many knots.

Doubling a knot

Doubling a knot gives it extra bulk, makes it more secure and also more decorative. Doubling simply means following the lay, or route, of the knot a second time with the rope, adding an extra circuit. Practise this yourself by tying a loose, first knot. Then take one end of the rope and thread it back into the start or finish of the knot. Keep the rope lying flat alongside the original 'path' of rope and follow the path of the knot until all of the parts of the knot have been doubled.

The differen
types of kno

Bend: fisherman's knot just before the two component overhand knots are drawn together.

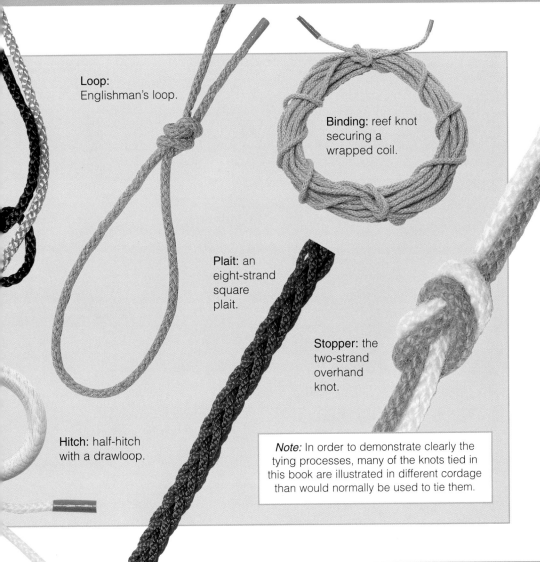

Loop:
Englishman's loop.

Binding: reef knot
securing a
wrapped coil.

Plait: an
eight-strand
square
plait.

Stopper: the
two-strand
overhand
knot.

Hitch: half-hitch
with a drawloop.

Note: In order to demonstrate clearly the
tying processes, many of the knots tied in
this book are illustrated in different cordage
than would normally be used to tie them.

WHIPPING
AND
COILING

Whipping is binding the ends of a rope to prevent the end from fraying. Whipping twines are sold by rope stockists, and you should use natural-fibre twine for whipping natural-fibre ropes and synthetic twine for synthetic ropes. Once whipped, the ends of synthetic ropes should not be heat-sealed. Keeping cordage in good condition is aided by coiling and securing it. This prevents tangling and makes the rope easy to untie.

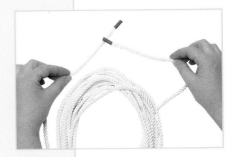

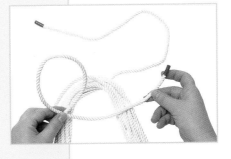

Alpine coil

This is a method of coiling and securing rope that is preferred by climbers and cavers. It's simple and effective and the coil can be easily transported over the shoulder or suspended safely in storage.

1 Bring the two ends of the coil rope close together.

2 Bend one end of the rope back to make a bight about 20cm (8 inches) long.

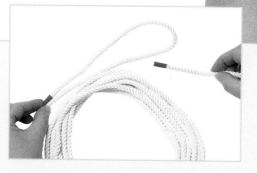

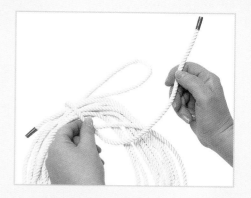

3 Wrap the other end of the rope around the bight and the coiled rope.

Make a second turn around the coil
and the bight, trapping the first turn.

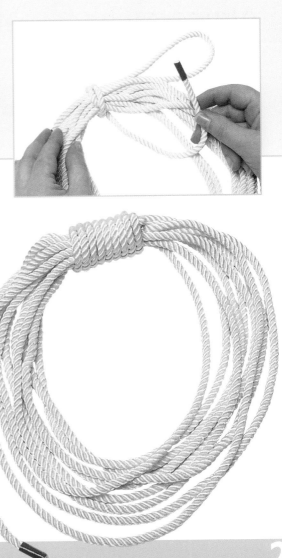

5 Make a succession of
turns, wrapping each
tightly and snugly against
the previous turn. Complete
at least six wrapping turns
and then tuck the working
end through the bight and
pull on the other end to
secure it.

Wrapped and reef knotted coil

This is a useful way of coiling and securing rope. The series of reef knots helps to ensure that the coil remains tangle-free when moved around. Use this method for storing rope in the boot of your car.

1 Bring the two fairly long ends of the coiled rope together and tie a half-knot – left over right and under.

Tie a second half-knot, this time going right over left and under.

3 Take the two ends away from the reef knot and wrap them around the coil with identical diagonal turns.

4 When the two ends meet at the opposite side of the coil to the reef knot, tie a half-knot – left over right and under.

5 Add a second half-knot, this time right over left and under, to make a second reef knot.

29

Fireman's coil

This method of securing a coil uses a hanging loop.

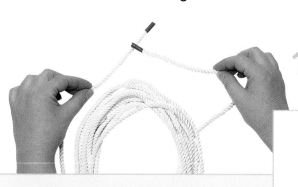

1 Bring the two ends of the coiled rope together.

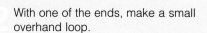

2 With one of the ends, make a small overhand loop.

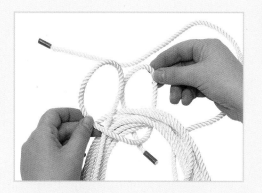

3 Pass the working end through the coil of rope and behind, and make a bight.

4 Tuck the bight through the loop from back to front and pull it tight.

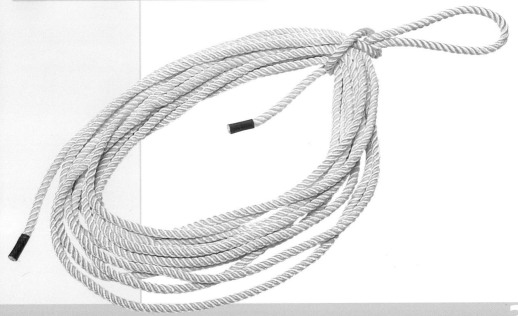

Common whipping

This method of whipping is quick to do but it is also the one most likely to come undone. Wrapping turns around the rope are made in the opposite direction to the lay of the rope: as the rope tries to unlay, the whipping becomes tighter.

Note: For demonstration purposes, thicker cord than is usually used for whipping has been used here.

1 Make a long bight in the whipping twine and lay it along the rope.

Wrap the working end of the whipping twine around the rope, trapping both legs of the bight with the first turn.

3 Continue to wrap tightly and evenly towards the end of the rope. Continue until the whipping is as long as the rope is wide.

4 Tuck the working end of the whipping twine through the remaining bit of the bight.

5 Pull the standing end to reduce the bight until it traps the working end.

6 Pull harder, so that the working end is dragged under the wrapping turns. Stop when the interlocked elbows reach the middle of the whipping and then trim the ends.

33

West-country whipping

This whipping is made by tying a series of half-knots on either side of the rope.

Tie an overhand knot about 2.5cm (1 inch) from the rope's end. (See page 38 for detailed instructions.)

2 Turn the rope over, face down, and tie an identical overhand knot on the reverse side.

3 Turn the rope face up again and tie a third overhand knot.

Turn the rope face down and tie a fourth overhand knot.

Repeat the process of knotting on alternate sides.

Finish with a reef knot– left over right and under, then right over left and under.

Poke the ends of the twine underneath the completed whipping. (You may need to use a pointed tool, like a small knitting needle or screwdriver.)

STOPPER KNOTS

Stopper knots are also known as knob knots, and are generally tied as a terminal knot in the end of a rope. Stopper knots are used to 'stop' the end of a length of rope, string or small stuff slipping through an eye or a hole. These types of knot can range from the simple to the elaborate: they include the knots that everyone has made to secure the ends of sewing thread and the decorative knob knots used to weight the ends of cords used for curtain tie-backs.

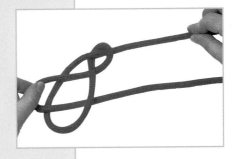

Overhand knot *(also known as thumb knot)*

The overhand knot is both the simplest of all knots and the basis of most other knots. In its own right, an overhand knot can be used as a simple stopper knot in the end of line. Sailors, in fact, rarely use this knot because it is a difficult one to untie when the rope is wet. Likewise, an overhand knot in small stuff like string can be difficult to undo.

1 Make a crossing turn by taking the working end of the small stuff behind the standing part.

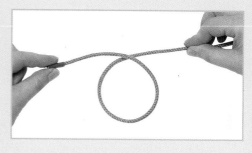

3 Pull on the working end and on the standing part to tighten the knot.

2 Tuck the working end through the loop that has already been formed.

Double overhand knot

This forms a bulkier stopper knot than the simple overhand knot. It can also be made even larger by adding more turns around the crossing turn.

1 Make a crossing turn by taking the working end of the small stuff behind the standing part.

2 Tuck the working end through the loop.

3 Tuck the working end a second time through the loop.

4 Pull tight on both ends of the rope and push the first turn into the centre of the knot.

Triple (and multiple) overhand knot *(also known as blood knot)*

Three or more tucks of the working end through the loop of a simple overhand knot will create this knot. The alternative name of 'blood knot' comes from the fact that this type of knot was tied in the ends of the lashes of a cat o' nine tails, the whip that was used for flogging in the British Royal Navy until it was banned in 1948. A less gruesome use is as a weight in the cords that monks and nuns use to tie their habits: the triple knot was a symbolic reference to their threefold sacred vows.

1 Follow steps 1 and 2 for the double overhand knot (see page 39).

2 Tuck the working end a third time through the loop. Keep the loop slack.

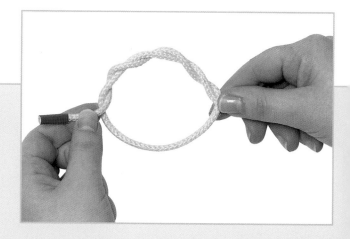

3 Pull on both ends of the rope, twisting them in opposite directions so that a diagonal wrapping turn appears.

4 Shape the knot with your fingers so that all of the turns lie snugly together.

5 Tighten the knot by pulling both ends of the rope.

Two-strand overhand knot

This is another of those knots that we all know how to tie. Once again it produces a bigger stopper knot and it is also used to hold together cords that are lying parallel to each other: it's the knot we use to tie together the two ends of sewing cotton after we've threaded a needle.

1 Place the two strings or cords to be tied parallel to each other.

2 Tie a simple overhand knot.

3 Taking care to keep the cords parallel, tighten the knot.

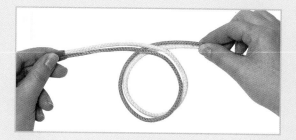

Slipped overhand knot

This is, in fact, a simple overhand knot with a drawloop. Drawloops act as quick releases, so this knot can be as easily untied as it can be tied. This knot can be tied either in the end or in the middle of a rope.

1 Make a crossing turn by taking the working end behind the standing part.

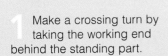

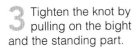

2 Double the working end to form a bight. Pass the bight through the crossing turn.

3 Tighten the knot by pulling on the bight and the standing part.

To release the knot, pull on the short working end.

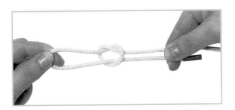

Overhand loop

This is a useful knot when a bulky stopper is needed. It is also the knot that most people use when they start tying string around a parcel. Because it doesn't untie easily, overhand loops generally have to be cut.

1 Double one end of the cord, i.e., make a bight in one end of a cord.

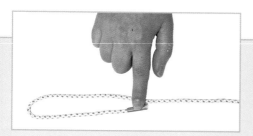

2 Form a loop in the bight.

3 Tie an overhand knot, taking care to keep the knot parts parallel throughout.

4 Tighten the knot by pulling on each of the four parts of the cord in turn.

Double overhand loop

Bigger and stronger than the single version, but don't try to untie it. Cut the knot off after use.

1 Make a long bight in the end of a cord.

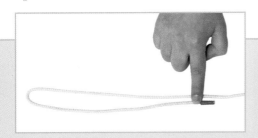

2 Tie a double overhand knot by passing the bight twice through the crossing turn.

3 Uncross any twisted knot parts and remove any slack, working the knot into shape.

4 Gradually tighten the knot by pulling on each of the four knot parts in turn.

Figure-of-eight knot

(also known as Flemish knot, Savoy knot)

This knot has long been used as a symbol of 'interwoven' affection. In heraldry it was used as the symbol of faithful love, and appears on the arms of the House of Savoy, giving rise to one of its alternative names. Sailors, however, use this knot widely on the running rigging – the ropes that are used to lift sails and yards. By tying a series of figure-of-eight knots, all in the same direction, you can also make a decorative chain.

1 Make a small bight at the end of a line.

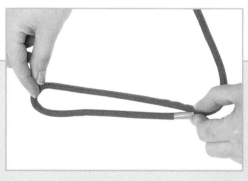

2 Give the bight a half-twist and turn it into a loop.

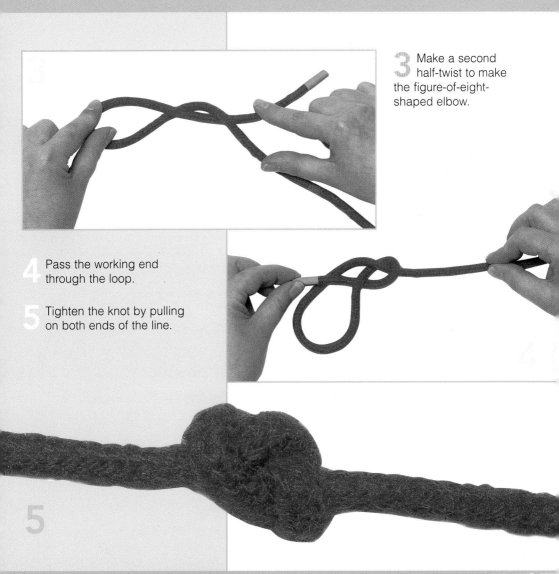

3 Make a second half-twist to make the figure-of-eight-shaped elbow.

4 Pass the working end through the loop.

5 Tighten the knot by pulling on both ends of the line.

Slipped figure-of-eight

This is a figure-of-eight knot but with a drawloop, so that the knot can be quickly untied by pulling on the working end.

1 Make a small bight at the end of a line.

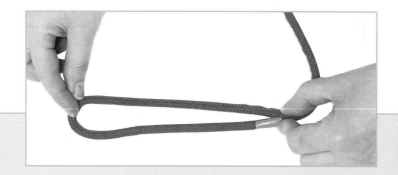

2 Give the bight a half-twist and turn it into a loop.

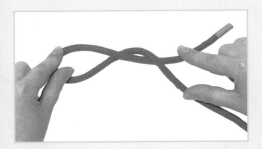

3 Make a second half-twist to make the figure-of-eight-shaped elbow.

4 Make a bight in the working end and pass it through the loop.

5 Pull the knot tight.

To release, pull on the working end of the rope.

LOOPS

A loop knot is a closed bight tied either in the end or in the central part of a rope. While it serves much the same purpose as a hitch, a loop is made to drop over an object, while a hitch is tied directly around an object and follows its shape. Consequently, hitches will undo or 'capsize' when removed from the object they are fastened to, while a loop can be used over and over again. Some loops are fixed into place, other loops are designed to slip and change size. These are called running knots, and have nooses that tighten around objects when tied and slacken when the strain is reduced.

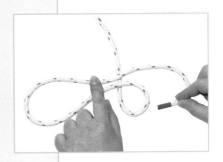

Bowline

A bowline (pronounced 'boh-linn') knot is one of the most used knots. It gets its name from the bow-line, a rope that held the weather-leech of a square sail forward – closer to the wind – and stopped the sail from being taken 'aback' – turned inside out. Today it is used for a variety of jobs because in normal conditions it never slips, loosens or jams.

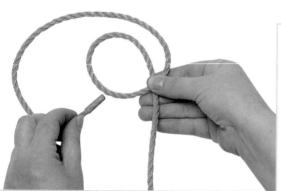

Form an overhand loop by bringing a long working end across the standing part of the rope and hold the crossing turn in place with one hand.

Take the working end through the crossing turn from front to back, leaving a long loop in the working end.

Take the working end
behind the standing part.

Pass the working end up
through the crossing turn
from front to back.

5 Tighten the
knot by
pulling on the
standing part
and the doubled
working end.

53

Double bowline

With an extra turn, this knot is stronger and more secure than the ordinary bowline.

1 Make an overhand loop with the working end lying on top of the standing part.

2 Make a second, identical loop on top of the first.

Hold the two loops together at the crossing turns.

4 Pass the working end through both loops from back to front, and leave a large loop in the working part of the rope.

5 Take the working end around behind the standing part.

6 Tuck the working end through the double loop from front to back. Tighten the knot by pulling on the standing part and the doubled working end.

55

Triple bowline

Used in climbing when proper harnesses are unavailable, this knot can be used to anchor oneself to a secure point, or as an improvised rescue sling. For rescue, the patient puts one leg through each of two loops, and their body through the third.

1 Middle a length of rope. (In a long climbing rope, you would make a long bight.)

Lay the working end of the bight over the standing part.

Bend the bight down and pass it through the twin loops from back to front.

4 Bring the bight up and trip the standing parts into the bowline form. The bight is now lying parallel to the standing parts. Adjust the twin loops to the required size.

5 Take the bight around the back of the standing parts.

6 Tuck the bight down from front to back, through the knot. The bight will form the third loop.

7 Grasp all of the legs of the loops firmly in one hand, and the two standing parts of the rope in the other hand, and pull in opposite directions.

57

Water bowline

Used in wet conditions the extra hitch provides additional security against jamming.

1 Form an overhand loop so that the working part lies on top of the standing part.

2 In the standing part of the rope, form a second overhand loop next to the first.

3 Make an extra tuck and then bring the ends together.

4 Pass the working end through the upper loop from back to front.

5 Take the working end around the back of the standing part.

6 Tuck the working end down next to its own standing part, through both the upper and lower loops.

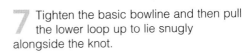 Tighten the basic bowline and then pull the lower loop up to lie snugly alongside the knot.

Spanish bowline *(also known as chair knot)*

This is another ancient knot also used in rescues, but the person being rescued needs to be fully conscious and aware of their actions. A leg is placed through each loop, and the person being rescued needs to hold on tight to the standing part of the rope at chest level, otherwise they will be tipped out.

1 Middle or make a long bight in the rope and then double it to make two twin loops.

2 Give the left-hand loop an anti-clockwise half-twist.

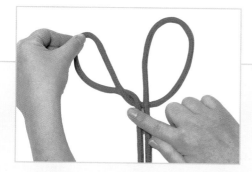

Now give the right-hand loop a clockwise half-twist.

Ensuring that the twists stay in place, pass the left-hand loop through the right-hand loop.

Rearrange the rope so that it follows the layout shown in the photograph. Ensure that the lines are parallel.

Make the lower crossing turn larger, producing two bights on either side of the standing parts of the rope.

Lift and twist both of the lower loops and pass them through the upper loops.

Pull the two loops outwards, until they reach the required size.

Tighten the knot by pulling down on the standing parts.

Portuguese bowline with splayed loops

This is a variation on another ancient mariner's knot. A pair of these knots, one at each end of a ladder, can make an improvised work platform or suspend a framework from which kitchen utensils can be hung. Note however, that each loop will pull slack from the other loop.

1 With the working end of the rope, form a crossing turn so that the working part lies on top of the standing part. Then, double back the working end to form a bight.

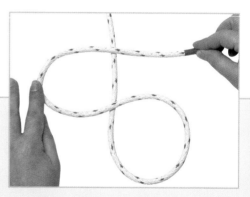

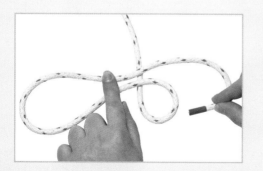

2 Reduce the size of the lower loop and hold on to the left-hand bight.

3 Bring the working end around to create a second loop and pass the working end through the small, central loop from back to front.

4 Now take the working end behind the standing part.

5 Tuck the working end down through the cinch of the central loop.

6 Adjust the two working loops to the required size and tighten the knot.

Bowline with stopper

For extra security, the working end of the rope is tied to the adjacent loop leg.

1 Tie a bowline, following steps 1–5 on pages 52–53.

2 Take the working end around the rope in the leg of the loop.

3 Tie an overhand knot through the crossing turn.

Surgeon's loop

Even stronger than the double version because of the extra turn, this loop is most often used by anglers, who tie it in extremely fine monofilaments.

1 Make a long bight in the end of a length of cord.

2 Form a loop in the doubled end.

3 Tie a treble overhand knot (see page 40).

4 Work out any unevenness in the body of the knot and work it into a smooth, barrel-shaped knot with your fingers.

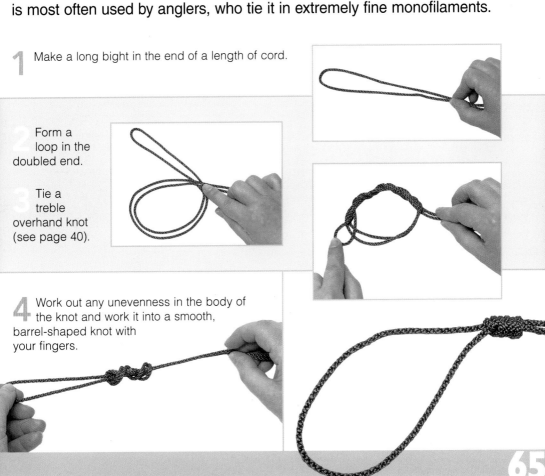

Arbor knot

An arbor is the alternative name for a reel or spool, and the knot is generally used by anglers to attach their monfilament to an arbor.

1 Make a bight in one end of a line.

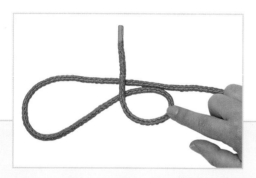

Form a small loop with the working end lying across the parallel parts of the line.

Bring the working end behind and then through the loop.

4 Take the working end over the two parallel parts of the line and then make a complete round turn.

5 Take the working end behind once more and make another complete round turn, keeping the wrappings tight as you turn.

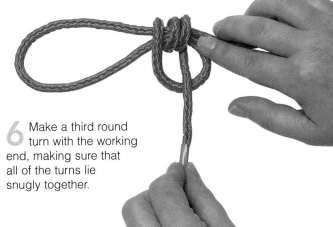

6 Make a third round turn with the working end, making sure that all of the turns lie snugly together.

7 Tighten the small loop and trap the end by pulling on one of the large loop legs.

Blood loop dropper knot

It is the twists in this knot that make it part of the 'blood knot' family (see Stopper knots: Double overhand knot, page 39.) This knot is generally tied at the end of fishing lines to form a loop to which a baited hook is fixed. It is also useful and attractive: the loop is formed in the middle of a line and can be used for all sorts of attachments.

1 Form a loop in the middle of the cord. (If you wish, thread an object like a key or a whistle on to the cord so that it will be suspended from this loop).

2 Tie a simple overhand knot (see page 38), keeping the loops quite loose.

3 Take a second tuck with either end of the cord. Again, keep the loops loose.

Take a third tuck. You have now made a triple overhand knot.

Find the centre of the two entwined knot parts.

6 Pull the original single loop down between the two knot parts, making a small bight.

7 Carefully shape the knot and work the turns together with the loop to the required size by pulling on the two standing parts.

69

Farmer's loop

This knot acquired its name in 1912, when Cornell University professor Howard W Riley described it in a pamphlet devoted to knots used on American farms. This is tied in a 'leap-frog' manner that produces a secure and strong knot. Once learnt, it's not easily forgotten.

In the place in the rope where the knot is required, wrap a complete turn around the hand from front to back.

2 Add another turn so that now there are three cord parts on both sides of your hand.

3 Pick up the middle cord and pass it over the right cord.

Find what is now the middle cord: this will be the loop of the farmer's knot.

Pull the loop into the required size and carefully tighten the knot.

4 Pick up the newly created middle cord and pass it over the left cord.

5 Pick up the new middle cord and pass this over to the right.

Frost knot

This knot is a recent 'invention': devised by Tom Frost during the 1960s. It is tied in order to create climbing ladders called étriers (French: stirrups).

Make a short bight at one end of a length of webbing.

Insert the other end between the two flat sections of the bight.

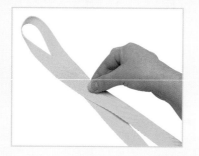

3 Make an anti-clockwise overhand loop with all three parts of the webbing.

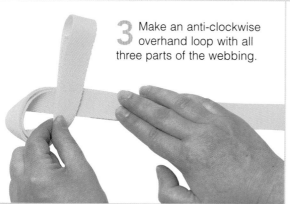

4 Take the bight, together with its extra end of webbing, around behind the loop and pull them all through. Making sure that all of the three sections are lying flat, tighten the knot.

Figure-of-eight loop

(also known as figure-of-eight on the bight, Flemish loop)

Hard to untie and tending to jam in wet natural-fibre ropes as it did, this knot was not favoured at sea. Nevertheless, because it is easily tied and can be checked quickly, it is a popular knot with climbers and speleologists – cavers and pot-holers – who use it to attach a line to a karibiner.

1 Make a long bight in the end of a length of cord or rope.

2 Take the bight over and behind the standing parts, making a crossing turn.

Bring the bight to the front of the knot and pass it through the loop made by the crossing turn. Pull the bight through the crossing turn. The bight will become the loop of the knot.

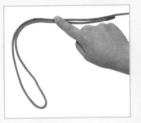

4 Pull on the bight the standing parts and open out the bight to make the loop.

Double Figure-of-eight loop

This knot is a little difficult to adjust and is not easily untied. It is, however, a very simple knot to tie – it is often used by climbers.

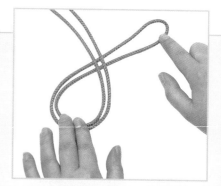

Where the knot is required, middle the rope. Make a clockwise underhand loop.

Bring the end of the bight over the standing parts of the rope from right to left.

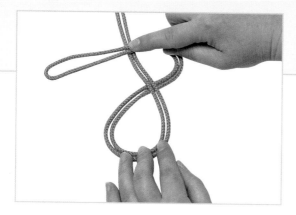

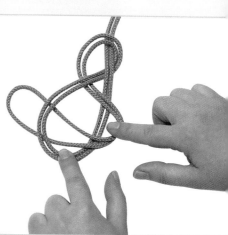

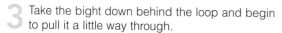
3 Take the bight down behind the loop and begin to pull it a little way through.

4 Adjust the forming loops to the required size.

5 Pass the bight over the pair of newly formed loops.

6 Take the bight all the way over the entire knot to secure the paired loops.

7 Tighten the knot by pulling on the standing parts of the rope and the pair of loops.

Double overhand sliding loop

This is a very useful knot around the house – try it for attaching cord to the arm of your reading or sun glasses and you'll never lose them again.

Make a crossing turn so that the working end lies underneath the standing part of the cord.

Take the working end around the crossing turn to complete a turn.

Take the working end around the crossing turn once more to create a second turn.

Insert the working end through the two turns.

5 Tighten the knot by pulling on the working end and the loop. Pull on the standing part to adjust the size of the loop.

You can make a multiple overhand sliding loop by adding as many turns as you like. This example shows four turns.

Simple noose

This is the simplest of all of the running (sliding) loops. Compare it with the overhand knot with a drawloop (page 43) and notice how this knot is tied in the standing part of the cord.

1 Hold the working end of a length of cord in one hand.

2 With your other hand, in the standing part of the cord, tie an overhand knot with a drawloop (see page 43).

3 To tighten the knot, pull on the loop.

Adjustable loop

This is a knot created by Canadian climber Robert Chisnall. Shock-loading will cause it to slide until friction reduces the load to a point when it will hold. Pull on the standing part of the rope and see for yourself!

1 Make a loop with the working end lying over the standing part of the rope.

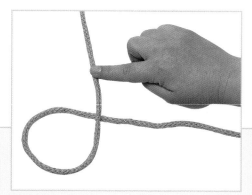

2 Take the working end and make a turn around the standing part.

3 Make a second turn around the standing part.

Pass the working end around both legs of the loop.

Tuck the working end underneath the second wrapping turn.

6 Tighten the knot by pulling on the loop and the working end, and then work it into shape.

Midshipman's hitch

A versatile knot that can be either temporary or permanent. It is useful for tensioning tent guy lines, also for binding, as it can be tightened and loosened easily around a package.

Make a clockwise overhand loop of about the required size.

2 Take the working end around and pass it through the loop just made.

3 Take the working end up and begin a wrapping turn that crosses and traps its own earlier turn.

4 Take the working end once more through the loop so that this second turn lies above the first.

5 Take the working end behind the standing part, outside the loop, and take it from left to right across the front of the standing part.

6 Make a half-hitch around the standing part and tighten it so that it lies alongside the other turns.

Tarbuck knot

This knot relies for its grip on the dog's leg made in the standing part of the rope. It is another useful knot for securing things around the house.

Make a loop of the required size with the working end lying over the standing part of the rope.

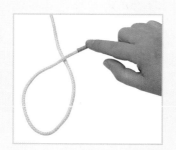

Tuck the working end down through the loop.

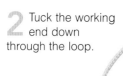

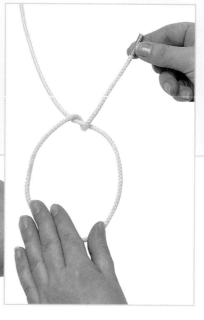

Bring the working end up through the loop and then start to make a second wrapping turn.

6 Bring the working end to the back of the standing part and then down through the middle loop.

4 Complete two turns around the standing part of the rope and then pass the working end behind the standing part.

5 Now bring the working end around the front of the standing part.

7 Tighten the knot little by little until all of the slack has been removed.

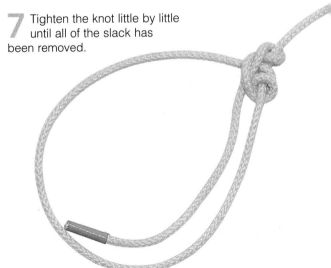

Tom Fool's knot

This is one of the many so-called 'handcuff' knots, but it's rather like the bow tied in shoelaces. Rather than restrain villains – although Clifford Ashley suggests that they may have originated with gamekeepers who used them to secure poachers – these knots were used to hobble farm animals so that they were free to graze but could not travel very far. Similar knots are still used today all over the Greek islands to keep goats in check – assuming that they haven't eaten through the rope.

1 Make a clockwise overhand loop in the bight of a length of rope.

2 Add an anti-clockwise underhand loop of about the same size.

3 Partly overlap the left-hand loop in front of the right-hand one.

5 Pull out the twin loops and adjust to the correct size.

4 Pull the leading edge of the left-hand loop (from the front to the back) through the right-hand loop and, at the same time, pull the leading edge of the right-hand loop (from the back to the front) through the left-hand loop.

6 Then tighten the knot.

Handcuff knot

A slight variation on the Tom Fool's knot, it's doubtful whether this version is any stronger, but it does make an attractive knot: try it on 'fat' shoelaces.

1 Make a clockwise overhand loop in the bight of a length of rope.

Add an anti-clockwise underhand loop of about the same size.

Partly overlay the right-hand loop in front of the left-hand one.

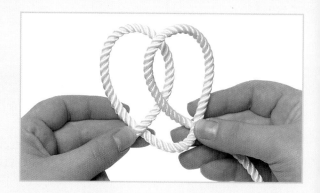

4 At the same time, pull the leading edge of the left-hand loop (from the back to the front) through the right-hand loop, and the leading edge of the right-hand loop (from the front to the back) through the left-hand loop.

Adjust the loops to the required size and then tighten the knot.

Fireman's chair knot

The handcuff knot is the basis for this more elaborate knot, which is, in fact, finished with a couple of half-hitches. As its name suggests, firefighters used this in rescues. One loop fitted under the victim's armpits, the other behind the knees. The rescuer then lowered the victim by means of one long end, while a second rescuer on the ground pulled the victim away from the wall or flames.

1 Make a clockwise overhand loop in the bight of a length of rope.

2 Add an anti-clockwise underhand loop of the same size.

Partly overlay the right-hand loop in front of the left-hand one.

4 At the same time, pull the leading edge of the left-hand loop (from the back to the front) through the right-hand loop, and the leading edge of the right-hand loop (from the front to the back) through the left-hand loop.

5 Adjust the loops to the required size and then tighten the knot.

6 Take the left-hand standing part around the back of the left-hand loop and bring it over to the front.

7 Take the working end down through its own loop to tie a half-hitch.

8 Take the right-hand standing part over the top of the right-hand loop and round the back.

9 Tuck the working end through its own loop from front to back to tie another half-hitch.

Hangman's noose *(also known as Jack Ketch's knot)*

No knot handbook would be complete without this knot! Its name reveals its macabre use, and its alternative name comes from the executioner Jack Ketch, who died in 1686. The number of turns can vary between seven (for the Seven Seas, perhaps) and 'unlucky' thirteen – although an odd number is always used.

> **Important:** As its name implies, this can be a very dangerous knot. DO NOT place it around the neck, even as a game.

1 In the end of a length of cord or rope, make a flattened-out 'S' or 'Z' shape.

With the working end, wrap the twin legs of the loop.

Make sure that the third part of the cord is trapped in the groove between the other two parts.

4 With the working end, continue to wrap the three enclosed knot parts, keeping each turn quite tight by pulling on the working end.

5 Continue to make seven wrapping turns in total – or more, as long as there is an odd number.

6 Tuck the working end through the small loop.

7 Trap the working end by pulling on whichever leg of the large loop closes the other small loop.

BINDING KNOTS

There are two kinds of binding knot: those that pass around an object one or more times, with the two ends of rope tied together, and those that pass around an object two or more times, with the ends of the rope tucked under the turns. Likewise, binding knots serve two purposes. Firstly, they either confine or constrict a single object or, secondly, they can hold together two or more objects. While whipping and seizing do much the same as binding knots, they are not considered binding knots because they have too many turns and are therefore more like lashings.

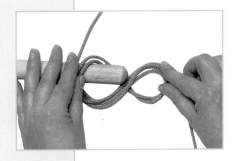

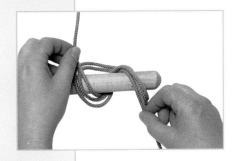

Reef knot

(also known as square knot, true knot, hard knot, flat knot and ordinary knot)

This is one of the oldest knots, and is also one that most people know how to tie. Known and used by civilisations as far back as the ancient Egyptians, the reef knot is unique in that it can be tied and tightened with both ends. The name reef knot comes from its nautical use: it was traditionally used to tie up a reef (sail). Today, we are most likely to use it around the home in tying up parcels. The simple way to remember how to tie a reef knot is: left over right and under, right over left and under.

> Note: Never use a reef knot as a bend: if tied with two ends of unequal size or stiffness, it is not secure. (See chapter on bends.)

1 Take the two ends of the same piece of cord. Place the left-hand end over the right-hand end.

2 Tie a half-knot by taking the left-hand end under and back up over the right-hand end.

3 Bring the two ends together and place the right-hand end over the left-hand one.

4 Tie a second half-knot by taking the right-hand end under and back up over the left-hand end.

5 Pull on the two ends to tighten the knot.

Surgeon's knot *(also known as ligature knot)*

This is a variation of the reef knot, and is used by surgeons to tie off blood vessels. It's the extra tuck that adds just enough friction to keep the knot in place until it has been completed.

1 Take the two ends of a length of cord or rope and then cross the left end over the right end.

2 Tie a half knot.

3 Make an extra tuck and then bring the ends together.

4 Tie a second half-knot, this time right over left.

5 Pull on one working end and its adjacent standing part, then pull on the other working end and its adjacent standing part.

6 Pull on the standing parts only, and let the upper half-knot twist slightly so that it overlays the completed knot from corner to corner.

You can make the surgeon's knot even more secure by adding a second tuck in the upper half-knot at the end of step 4.

Granny knot

(also known as false knot, booby knot and lubber's knot)

This has to be the most widely used knot. With twin drawloops, it's the knot we use to tie our shoelaces with – and it's the knot that most often lets our shoelaces come undone. It's a pretty unreliable knot, as it either slips or jams – the sort of knot tied by a 'land lubber'! Compare this knot with the reef knot, which is more secure because its two knot parts spiral in opposite directions, as opposed to the granny knot, both of whose half-knots are tied in the same direction. (The granny knot mnemonic is: left over right and under, left over right and under.)

1 Take the two ends of a piece of cord and bring them together, crossing the left-hand end over the right-hand one.

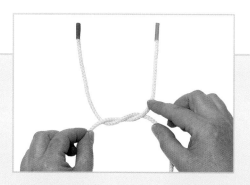

2 Tie a half-knot by passing the left-hand end under and back up over the right-hand end.

3 Bring the ends together again, and now cross the left-hand end over the right-hand end.

4 Tie a second half-knot by passing the left-hand end under and back up over the right-hand end.

5 Tighten the knot by pulling on both ends.

True lover's knot

Tied using two lengths of rope and made up of two separate overhand knots, each mirroring the other, this binding knot is often regarded as symbolic of the binding love between two people. It looks most effective when tied in ropes of different colours.

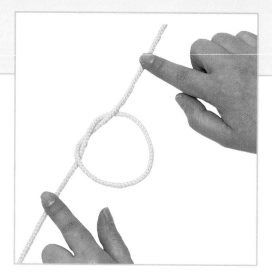

1 Tie an overhand knot in a length of rope, keeping the loop fairly loose.

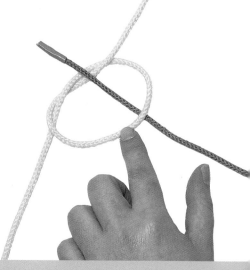

2 Pass the working end of the second length of rope up through the loop.

3 Bring the working end of the second rope over its own standing part to make a crossing turn.

4 Tie a second overhand knot by tucking the working end of the second rope through the crossing turn.

5 Pull on the ends of both ropes to tighten the knot.

Thief knot *(also known as bread-bag knot)*

At first glance, this knot looks very similar to a reef knot, but, in fact, it is tied so that the short ends are on opposite sides. Legend has it that sailors tied up their kit bags containing clothes or foodstuffs – hence 'bread-bag knot' – with this knot, but thieves would retie the knot using a granny knot, thereby revealing that a theft had taken place.

1 Make a small bight in one end of the cord.

2 Pass the other end of the cord through the bight just made, angling it towards the short end of the bight.

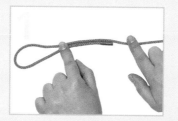

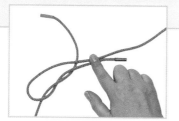

3 Take the working end of the cord around the back of both parts of the bight.

4 Tuck the working end back through the bight so that it emerges and lies alongside its own standing part.

Grief knot *(also known as whatknot)*

This has a similar formation to the granny knot, except that the ends are diagonally opposite each other. Like the granny and thief knots, the grief knot is not a very secure knot, but with the ends pulled tightly it could be used to bind lightweight structures made of garden canes.

1 Make a bight in one end of the cord.

2 Tuck the working end up through the bight just made, angling it towards the other short end.

3 Tuck the working end under the short leg of the bight and then over the standing part of the bight.

4 Tuck the working end back once more through the bight to emerge from the completed knot alongside its own standing part.

Transom knot

This is the knot that every child wishes that they knew. It was originally devised by Clifford Ashley to hold together the two cross sticks of his daughter's kite. A secure knot – it is 'related' to the constrictor knot – try using it in the garden for securing trelliswork.

1 Lay the objects to be secured– in this instance, bamboo poles – at right angles: the horizontal lying on top of the vertical.

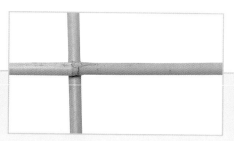

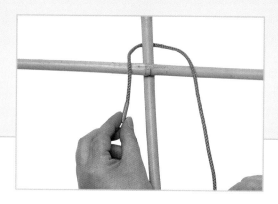

2 Take the working end of the cord over the horizontal pole and around the back of the vertical pole.

3 Bring the working end diagonally down and across its own standing part.

4 Take the working end around the back of the vertical piece and return it to the front.

5 Tuck the working end under and through the diagonal knot part to form a half-knot.

6 Pull on the ends to tighten. If additional strength is required, a second transom knot can be tied at the back of the crossed poles, at right angles to the knot on the front.

Pole-lashing

Here is a very simple way to secure any number of long objects together. It can keep garden canes or tent poles tidy for storage so that you've always got the complete set! Tied 'head-to-handle', it's surprising how many tennis, badminton or squash racquets can be made to behave themselves.

Arrange the cord in an 'S' shape underneath, and close to, the end of the objects to be tied together.

Take one end of the cord over the objects and down through the bight that it was directly opposite.

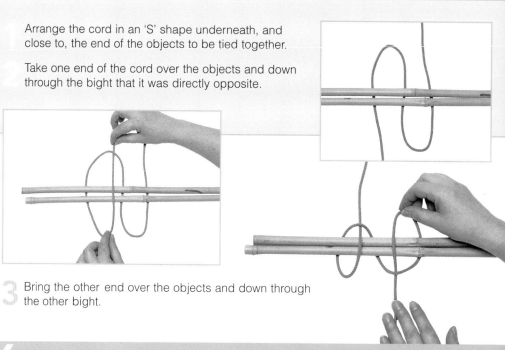

Bring the other end over the objects and down through the other bight.

4 Pull both ends of the cord to draw the cord and objects snugly together.

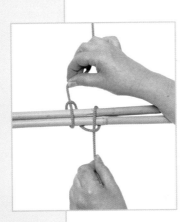

5 Cross the two ends over, left end over right end, and pull tight.

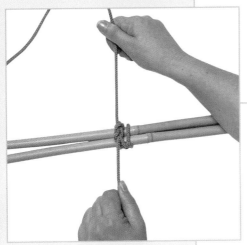

6 Bring the ends back together and cross them over, right end over left end, to complete the reef knot.
With a second length of cord, repeat these steps at the other end of the objects.

Plank sling

A relative of pole-lashing, but
use rope rather than cord for
extra strength.

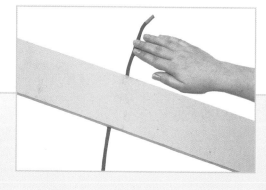

1 Place one end of the rope underneath
the plank.

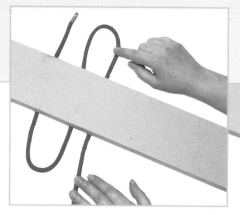

2 Push an extra bight underneath the plank
to make an 'S' shape.

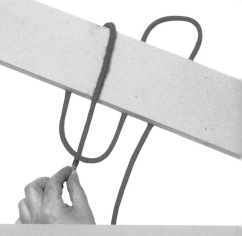

3 Bring one end of the rope over the plank and
tuck it through the bight on the opposite side
of the plank.

4 Take the other end of rope over the plank and tuck it through its opposite bight.

5 Adjust and tighten the sling so that the tips of the bights are positioned just above the edge of the plank.

6 The object can now be suspended for storage.

Constrictor knot

This is one of the best of the binding knots. It can be tied in the end or on a bight, and is a difficult knot to untie: to remove a constrictor knot, carefully sever the overriding diagonal with a sharp knife, taking care not to cut or scar whatever lies underneath it. Clifford Ashley suggests using this knot to secure a cork to the neck of a bottle, to tie to a broom handle to allow it to be suspended, and to hold the fuse tight in a stick of dynamite! In short, this knot has a thousand-and-one uses. Use a stiff cord to bind soft, yielding objects, such as rope, and soft, 'stretchy' cord for harder objects.

Tied in the bight

This method of tying a constrictor knot is useful when the end of the foundation rope or other object is accessible – for instance, the end of a broom handle.

1 Take the working end of a short length of cord or twine from front to back over the foundation rope or object.

2 Lift the working end to complete a full turn.

3 In the lower part of the turn just made, pull down a fairly long bight.

4 Lift the bight and give it a half-twist.

5 Pass the bight over the end of the foundation object.

6 Pull tightly (as tightly as the cord or twine will allow without breaking) on both ends. Trim off the ends close to the knot.

111

Constrictor Knot tied in the end

1 Take a short length of cord or twine and arrange it around the object to be tied.

2 Bring the working end of the cord up and across to the right, over its own standing part.

3 Take the working end down at the back and up once more at the front.

4 Tuck the working end underneath the diagonal made earlier, completing a clove hitch.

Find, and then slightly loosen, the upper left-hand knot part.

6 Bring the working end across and tuck it from left to right through the loosened bight.

7 Tighten the knot by pulling both ends in opposite directions. If using very thin stuff to tie, it helps to wrap the ends around the end of two sticks. That way you'll get a better 'pull' without cutting off the circulation (or worse) in your fingers.

8 Cut off the knot ends quite close to the knot.

Boaknot

For a binding knot that is decorative, as well as practical, the boa knot is quick and easy to tie.

1   In a short length or cord or rope, make an overhand loop.

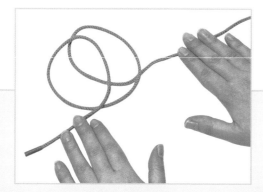

2   Add a second turn on top of the first one.

3   Arrange these loops in the form of a coil, with both ends lying in the same direction. You should have three cord parts under each thumb.

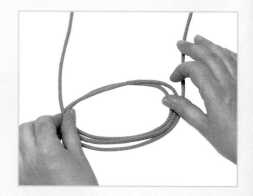

4 Lift the three cord parts on the right-hand side and rotate them through 180°. (Make sure that the resulting figure of eight has three strands around each loop and on the top overlying diagonal, with just two strands beneath it.)

5 Insert the end of the pole, rope or other object beneath one of the end loops.

6 Slide the pole, rope or other object over the centre crossing and push it carefully through the other loop.

7 Work the knot into shape and pull on the ends to tighten it.

Double figure-of-eight hitch

An alternative to both the boa and constrictor knots, this is an easy-to-remember, figure-of-eight binding knot.

1 Make a clockwise overhand loop with one end of a length of cord.

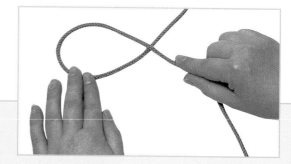

2 Add an anti-clockwise overhand loop to form a figure of eight.

3 Lay a second clockwise overhand loop on top of the first one.

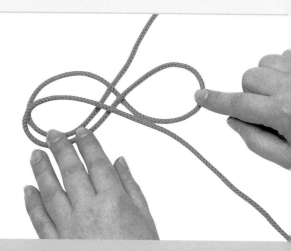

4 Pick up the other end of the cord and lay a second anti-clockwise overhand loop on top of the first.

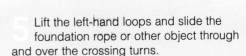

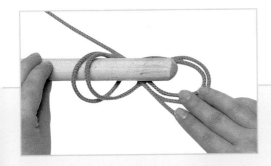

5 Lift the left-hand loops and slide the foundation rope or other object through and over the crossing turns.

6 Lift the right-hand loops and slide the foundation rope or other object through.

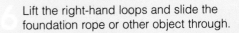

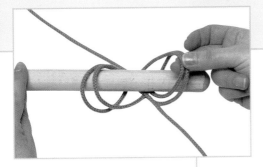

7 Place the knot in the position required on the foundation rope and pull on both ends to tighten.

Square Turk's head *5 lead x 4 bight*

The Turk's head is a tubular knot that is usually tied around a cylindrical object. While the knot serves a variety of practical uses, because it's so attractive it is often used purely for decoration. This is a beautiful-looking knot, especially when tied in natural cordage. Make a key fob or attach the knot to anything you want to single out as special or mark as your own. The knot has interwoven strands (or leads), with scallop-shaped rim parts (bights), and the numbers of each are given a shorthand: 2 lead x 3 bight; 3 lead x 4 bight. Try this version of the Turk's head by tying it on your hand before slipping it over the designated object.

1 Middle a length of cord and pass the working end over and down behind your hand, letting it reappear on the right of the standing part. Bring up the standing end diagonally, from right to left, over the previous lead.

2 Take the working end over, around and down behind your hand, emerging to the immediate right of the standing part. Then, from right to left, tuck the working end over, then under, then over.

Take the working end down behind your hand, letting it reappear again to the right of the standing part and, working from left to right, tuck it under, then over.

Rotate the work so that you can now see the rear side and tuck the end on this side from right to left, over, then under, then over.

Turn the work back to its original position. Take the working end to the right of the standing part and tuck it from left to right, over, then under, then over.

Rotate the work to show the rear side again. Lead this end from right to left in a final locking tuck, going under, over, under and over.

Place the working end alongside the standing part to complete the knot or, if you wish, you could double, or even treble, the knot by following around the original lead with the surplus cord.

Slide the knot over the core object, work the shape and tighten the knot. Be patient, as this can take time.

HITCHES

Hitches are knots that are used to secure a rope to a post, hook, ring, rail or to another rope that plays no part in the actual tying. A line or rope is said to be 'made fast' rather than 'hitched', because only the knot itself is called a hitch. Some hitches work when the pull is at right angles, such as when a rope is made fast to a rail. Others will withstand a lengthways pull, as with making fast to rigging, masts and cables.

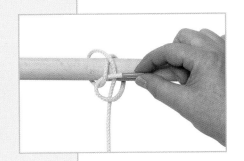

Half-hitch *(also known as single hitch)*

This is one of the most widely used temporary fastenings, even though on its own it is also one of the most unreliable! It is best used to finish off other, more substantial, hitches, since a half-hitch is not meant to take any strain.

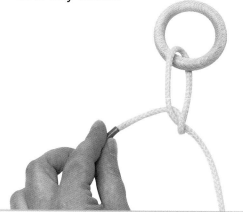

1 Around something firm – a curtain ring or broomstick, for example – tie an overhand knot.

If you leave a slightly longer working end, you can add a drawloop by not pulling the working end completely through the knot.

Two half-hitches

Adding a second, identical half-hitch makes
for a much more secure fastening.

1 Around something firm,
tie a single half-hitch
(an overhand knot).

2 Make a loop.

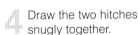

3 Add a second, identical half-hitch – make sure that
the working end goes around the standing part in
the same direction as the first.

4 Draw the two hitches
snugly together.

Round turn and two half-hitches

This is a useful knot for attaching a washing line, mooring a boat and even towing a broken-down car. It can take a great deal of strain, but can be easily untied.

1 Pass the working end of a line from back to front, through or around the anchorage.

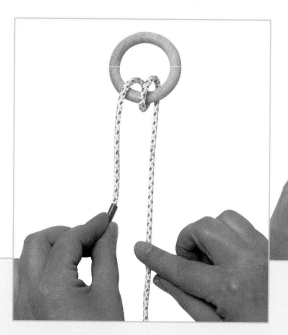

2 Pass the working end around or through a second time, to form a round turn.

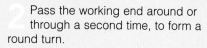

3 Take the working end across, then behind, the standing part and pass it through the knot to tie a half-hitch.

4 Now make an identical half-hitch.

5 Pull on both rope parts to tighten the knot.

Add an extra round turn at step 2 to make two round turns and two half-hitches, and you will have a great knot for fastening rope to a strong tree limb to make a swing.

Overhand knot and half-hitch

(also known as packer's knot)

A useful knot for starting to tie parcels, or, in the kitchen, to tie up boned and rolled joints of meat.

1 Tie an overhand knot with a large drawloop. Adjust the drawloop to the required size.

2 Tie a half-hitch, with the working end around the standing part.

3 Tighten the knot by pulling on each leg of the loop in turn.

Crossing knot

Possibly the simplest and the most insecure of all hitches, this is nevertheless a useful one: we use it all the time when we tie a parcel, and it is also the basis of the harness bend. This is a quick and useful way of 'roping off' an enclosure, but because there is no locking tuck to hold it, tension on the line must be maintained.

1 Cross one line over another so that they are at right angles to each other.

2 Bring the working end of the line down, behind the other line.

3 Take the working end across the front of its own standing part.

4 Tuck the working end up and under the other line.

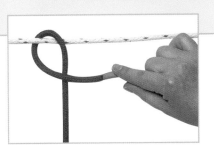

Ossel hitch

Ossel is the Scottish word for a gill net (at the other end of Britain, in Cornwall, it's called an orsel). This is a very simple, yet very effective, knot.

1 Pass the working end of the line down behind the foundation object or rope and up to the front.

2 Pass the working end around the back of the standing part.

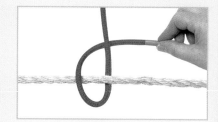

3 Bring the working end down in front of the foundation object and back up behind it.

4 Tuck the working end over the first knot part and then underneath the second.

Sheepshank

This well-known knot is designed to shorten a rope without cutting it. It is also useful for taking the strain off a worn part of rope by positioning the damaged area in the centre of the knot.

1 Make three crossing turns, all in the same direction along the line.

2 Pull the central crossing turn through the back of the right-hand crossing turn and through the front of the left-hand crossing turn.

3 Pull on the newly formed loops and then on the standing parts.

Note: A sheepshank will only hold if the strain is applied to the standing parts.

Ossel knot

This is a more secure version of the ossel hitch.

1 Pass the working end of the line from front to back, over the foundation object or rope.

2 Bring the working end up, and diagonally across, in front of the standing part and then back down behind the foundation object.

3 Bring the working end up alongside the diagonal crossing turn and take a second wrapping turn around the object and the standing part.

4 Take another turn up and around the foundation object, this time without trapping the standing part.

5 Where the standing part passes over the top of the foundation object, pull out a bight.

6 Tuck the working end, working from front to back, through the bight.

7 Trap the working end by pulling down on the standing part.

Pedigree-cow hitch

This is a useful knot for suspending garden tools from the roof of a shed or outhouse.

1 Over the anchor point/object, take the working end of a line around and down, from front to back.

2 Bring the working end around and across the front of its own standing part.

3 Take the working end back up behind the anchor point/object and then down in front once more.

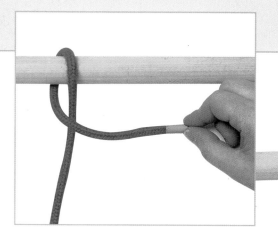

4 Tuck the working end through the bight.

5 Tuck the working end back through the knot.

Major Turle's knot

(also known as Turle knot, and sometimes turtle knot)

Major Turle, of Hampshire, England, popularised this knot as an angler's knot during the mid-nineteenth century. It is a useful knot for tying through objects which have an 'eye', or hole, which can then be suspended and stored.

1 Pass the working end of the line through the eye of the object.

2 Take the working end around the shank, or neck, of the object and across the standing part to make a loop.

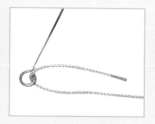

3 Tuck the working end through the loop to make a half-hitch.

4 With the working end, tie an overhand knot.

Palomar knot

This is a very strong knot that is used by fishermen to tie a line to a hook when there is likely to be a great deal of strain.

1 Double the end of a line to make a bight and then pass it from front to back through the ring.

2 Bring the bight back across itself and then tuck it through the loop formed to tie an overhand knot.

3 Push the ring down through the bight.

4 Take the bight all the way over the knot parts.

Jansik special

Another very strong hitch, it is the double turn through the ring that gives it strength, while the triple tuck makes it secure. Fishermen tie this in nylon monofilament, but it's worthwhile practising it first using thicker cord.

1 Pass the working end of the line from back to front, through the ring and then under the standing part.

2 Take the working end through the ring a second time to create a round turn.

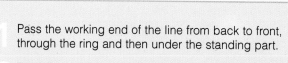

3 Take the working end under the standing part.

4 Take the working end over the two turns to make a wrapping turn.

5 Tuck the working end through the loop. Wrapping away from the ring, make a second wrapping turn.

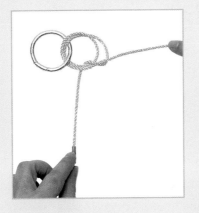

6 Complete three or four turns and then carefully remove the slack to tighten the knot.

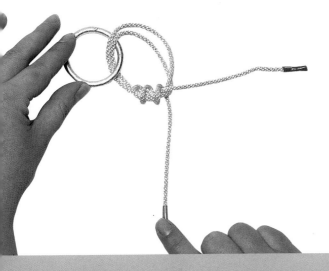

Prusik knot

This hitch is named after Dr Carl Prusik, who devised it to mend the broken strings of musical instruments. It's quite a simple knot to tie, and is much used by climbers to attach slings to a rope. The knot will slide smoothly when loose, but when a sideways strain is applied it will hold firm. This is the basis of all locking (slide-and-grip) knots.

Note: For safety reasons, this knot should be tied in thinner line than the rope to which it will be attached. It is also important to note that the knot may slip in wet or icy conditions.

1 Open out a loop at one end of a sling and lay the loop on top of the main rope.

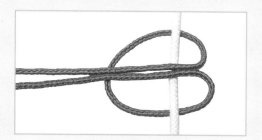

2 Bend the bight over and down behind the main climb rope.

3 Pass the standing part of the sling through the working bight.

4 Take the bight up and over once more.

5 Take the working bight back down behind the climbing rope.

6 Take the remainder of the standing part through the wrapped bight.

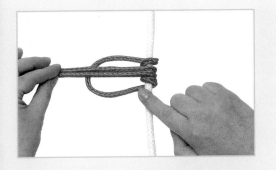

7 Tighten the knot.

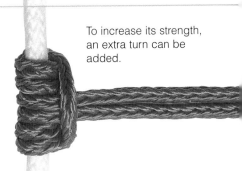

To increase its strength, an extra turn can be added.

Klemheist knot

This is a variation on the Prusik knot. The second rope used must be at least half the diameter of the main rope. This knot is used when downward/diagonal strain will be used – for example, placing a foot into a loop to begin climbing.

Note: Check and test the knot for security before using it to take any strain. Remember, too, that the knot will be less secure in wet or icy conditions.

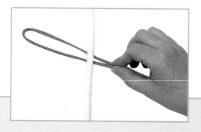

1 Make a bight in a sling and lay it behind the main rope.

2 Wrap the bight around the main rope in an upwards direction (as though it were 'climbing up' the rope).

3 Continue to wrap the sling upwards, along the main rope, making sure that both legs of the sling stay flat and parallel.

4 Complete four or five turns around the main rope.

5 Tighten the turns and bring the working bight down to the tail of the sling.

6 Tuck the tail of the sling through the working bight. To lock the knot in position, pull downwards on the tail of the sling.

Highwayman's hitch *(Also known as draw hitch)*

This is one of those knots that looks very complex when tied, but that seemingly magically disappears when the working end is pulled. This quick-release knot was supposedly used by highwaymen and robbers to tether their horses to ensure a rapid getaway.

1 Make a bight in one end of a line and pass it up behind the hitching rail.

2 Pick up the standing part of the line and make a similar bight in front of the rail.

3 Tuck the second bight, from front to back, through the first bight.

4 Pull on the working end to secure the hitch.

5 Make another bight in the working end (you have now made three bights in total).

6 Tuck the third bight from front to back, through the second bight. Pull on the standing part to secure.

To undo the hitch, give the working end a quick pull.

Halter hitch

Like the highwayman's hitch, this hitch is used to tether animals.

1 Take the working end of the line through, or around, the anchor point, so that it crosses its own standing part and forms a loop.

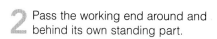

2 Pass the working end around and behind its own standing part.

3 Make a bight in the working end and tuck it through, forming a running overhand knot with a drawloop.

4 Tighten the knot and adjust the sliding loop.

5 Tuck the working end through the drawloop to secure it.

Pile hitch

As easy and quick to tie as it is to undo, this hitch is remarkably secure. It is ideal for attaching ropes to posts or rails, because the loop can be passed over the top.

1 Make a bight in the line.

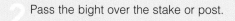
2 Pass the bight over the stake or post.

3 Bring the bight round the front of the stake or post and under both standing parts.

4 Loop the bight over the stake or post.

The two legs of the line can now be led off in different directions.

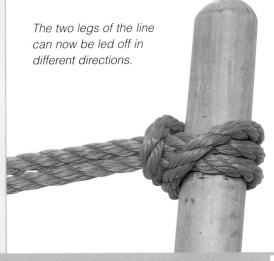

Double pile hitch

This double version will withstand loads on one or both of the standing parts.

1 Make a bight in the line.

2 Pass the bight over the stake or post.

3 Bring the bight round the front of the stake or post and under both standing parts.

4 Take the bight around the stake or post once more to make a turn.

5 Bring the bight up over the two standing parts and loop it over the stake or post.

Fisherman's bend (also known as anchor bend)

In spite of its name, this is actually a hitch. 'Bend' comes from the fact that sailors 'bent' a rope to an anchor or spar, and the knot is widely used to moor a boat at a quayside, since it is secure in wet or slippery ropes.

1 Leave a long working end of the line and pass it twice through the ring to form a round turn.

2 Bring the working end down and behind the standing part.

3 Tuck the working end through the round turn to form a locking half-hitch around the standing part.

4 Tie an identical half-hitch.

5 Tighten the knot by pulling on the working end and standing part.

For a semi-permanent hitch, tape or tie the working end to the standing part of the line.

Rolling hitch *(also known as Magner's hitch, Magnus hitch)*

This useful knot is used by mountaineers and mariners, and is the most effective way of securing a small rope to a larger line that is under strain. As long as the smaller rope is perpendicular to the larger rope, the knot will slide. But once tension is exerted on the standing part and working end of the smaller rope, the knot locks into position.

1 Pass the working end of the smaller line from front to back around the anchorage.

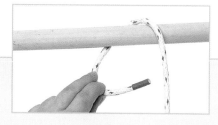

2 Take the working end up, and diagonally across, the front of the standing part.

3 Bring the working end down behind the anchorage once more and then out, so that it emerges between the diagonal and the standing part.

Make a second diagonal turn beside the first one and bring the working end behind the anchorage again.

Tuck the working end up through the second diagonal turn.

Pull on the working end and the standing part to tighten.

Boom hitch

This is a similar hitch to the rolling hitch, but is a little more decorative.

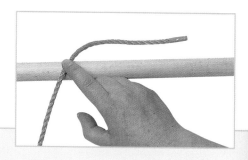

1 Lay the working end of the line over and diagonally across, from left to right, the rail or other anchor point.

2 Take the working end down behind the rail, then under and diagonally across its own standing part, working from right to left.

3 Take the working end down behind the rail once more and back to the front.

4 Take the working end diagonally across, from left to right, over the knot part.

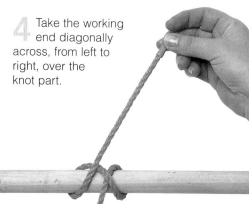

5 Take the working end between the two knot parts, then behind the rail and then up to the front of the rail.

6 Take the working end diagonally from right to left over the standing part and one knot part.

7 Take the working end over the rail once more and bring it out at the front.

8 Take the working end diagonally across, from left to right, going over one knot part and then under the next.

9 Pull on both rope parts to tighten and work the knot into shape.

Vibration-proof hitch

This hitch was devised by American physicist Amory Bloch Lovins. It's a very useful hitch to know, because any vibrations on the standing part of the line will tighten the knot even more.

1 Pass the working end of the line around the anchor point, from front to back.

2 Bring the working end diagonally up and to the right, underneath its own standing part.

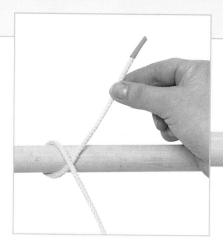

3 Take the working end up, over and down the back of the object once more.

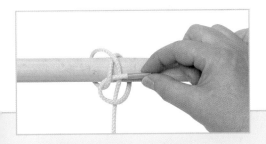

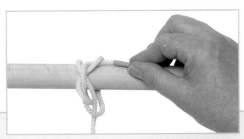

4 Take the working end across the front of its standing part and up through the underlying diagonal crossing, from left to right.

5 Take the working end over the overlying knot part and tuck it underneath the diagonal once more.

6 Tighten the knot by tugging on the standing part.

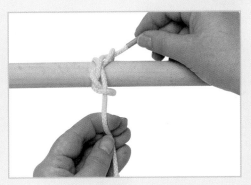

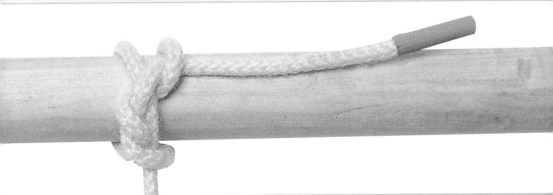

Clove hitch *(tied in a bight)*

Use this version of the clove hitch when the rope is not under strain. It's then possible to drop it over a bollard or to slip it on to the end of a rail. With practice, it should be possible to tie this knot with just one hand – very useful in rough weather, when you have to tie up to a bollard while holding onto a guard rail!

1 Make an overhand loop in the line.

2 Add an underhand loop further along the line.

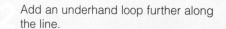

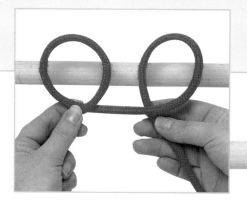

3 Arrange the loops so that they are of equal size and close together.

4 Slide the right-hand loop over the left-hand loop so that they overlap.

5 Slip the two loops over the rail or spar and pull on both ends of the rope to tighten the knot.

6 Work the clove hitch into shape to complete it.

Clove hitch *(tied with a working end)*

(also known as boatman's knot or peg knot)

This is a good knot for securing a boat to a bollard. Campers will also find this knot useful for securing their tent poles - hence one of the knot's alternative names.

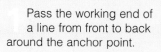

1 Pass the working end of a line from front to back around the anchor point.

2 Bring the working end up and diagonally across the front of the standing part.

3 Take the working end down behind the back of the anchorage to trap the standing part.

4 Tuck the working end up beneath the diagonal crossing. Pull on the standing part to tighten the knot.

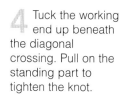

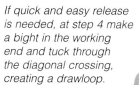

If quick and easy release is needed, at step 4 make a bight in the working end and tuck through the diagonal crossing, creating a drawloop.

Sheepshank man o' war

More secure and more decorative than the ordinary sheepshank, you may need to work the knot a little to make it regular.

1 Make four overlapping crossing turns in the same direction.

2 Pull the right centre strand through the right outer turn from back to front, and the left centre strand through the left outer turn from front to back.

3 Pull on the newly formed loops and then on the standing parts.

Ground-line hitch

Used to attach a thin line to a thicker one, this is the standard knot used by fishermen trawling for cod, but it was also used to hitch horses to picket lines.

1 Pass the working end of the line from front to back around the foundation object or thicker rope. Bring the working end forward and to the left of its own standing part.

2 Take the working end up and diagonally across the front of the standing part and foundation object.

3 Pass the working end down behind the foundation object so that it emerges at the front and to the right of the standing part.

4 Pull up on the standing part to create an upper bight.

5 Tuck the working end through the bight.

6 Pull down on the standing part to trap the working end and complete the knot.

Cat's paw

The cat's paw is a common hook hitch for slings, and is useful on wet or slippery rope. The double parts of loaded rope lessen the chances of the rope breaking, but if one leg should break, the other leg should be sufficient to lower the load to the ground.

1 Make a bight by doubling a length of rope.

2 Bring the end of the bight down over the standing parts to make a pair of matching loops.

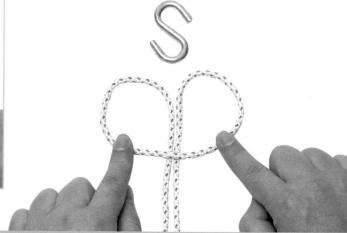

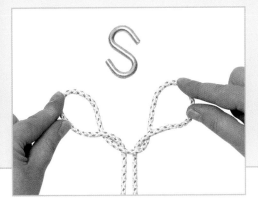

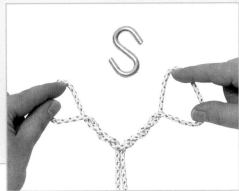

3 Give each loop a twist: the left-hand loop clockwise; the right-hand loop anti-clockwise.

4 Add two or three more twists to each loop.

5 Insert the hook or anchorage through both of the twisted loops.

6 Pull on the standing parts of the rope to straighten them and slide up the wrapping turns until they lie snugly against the hook or anchorage.

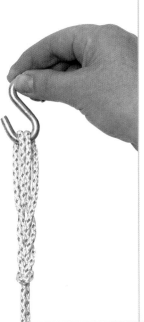

Marlinespike hitch

Originally, this hitch was used by sailors to pull on thin line or rope without it biting into their hands. Instead of a marlinespike, any long tool, such as a spanner, can be used, as demonstrated here. Once the knot is no longer needed, simply remove the tool and watch the hitch disappear.

1 Lay the spanner on top of a length of rope that has been fixed at one end.

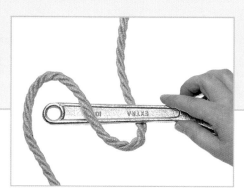

2 Lift the rope upwards and over the spanner.

3 Twist the spanner upwards, in a clockwise direction, and insert its head behind the standing part.

4 Open out the turn to cover both sides of the standing part.

5 With the head of the spanner, pull the standing part through the crossing turn.

6 Push the spanner further through the knot and, with one or both hands, apply strain to the rope by pulling down on both sides of the spanner.

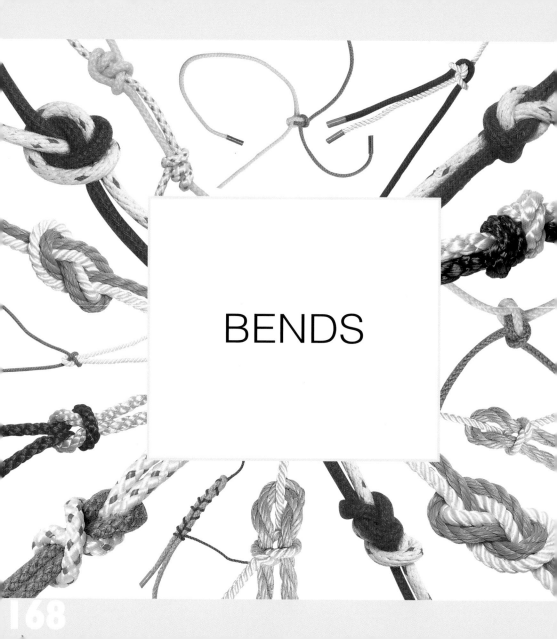

BENDS

A bend is a knot that unites two ropes, or two parts of the same rope, usually at the ends. Its purpose is to form one longer piece of rope, and it should ideally be possible to untie bends after use, particularly in valuable rope. However, in small stuff, like string, a bend that is a permanent fixture may well be desirable – for securely tying a parcel, perhaps. Where the material is only to be used once, the bend can be cut off and discarded. To ensure a secure bend, the ropes that are to be joined should be of the same diameter. Unusually, the sheet bend is secure, even when it is used to join different-sized ropes, and is therefore a very useful knot to know.

Double overhand bend

(also known as thumb knot, openhand knot, tape knot and water knot)

A good knot for tying together two ropes of the same thickness. Often used to tie webbing, it is very strong but quite difficult to untie.

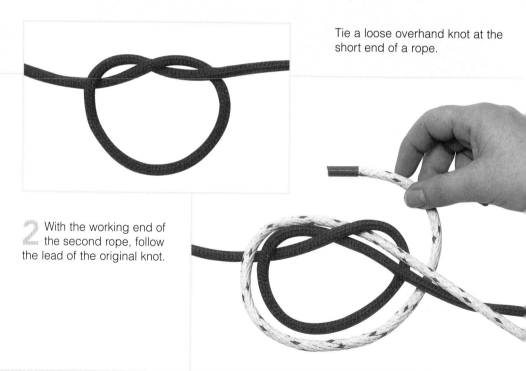

Tie a loose overhand knot at the short end of a rope.

2 With the working end of the second rope, follow the lead of the original knot.

3 Making sure that all parts remain parallel, continue passing rope through. Ensure that both short ends emerge at the top of the knot.

Tuck the working end under itself, making sure that both short ends are situated on the same side of the knot. Pull on the rope parts to tighten the knot.

Sheet bend *(also known as common bend and flag bend)*

This is an unusual bend, in that it can be tied using two different-diameter ropes. It is not, however, a secure knot, and can work loose if the rope is jerked about too much. It should therefore never be used in circumstances where great strain is put on the rope. Representations of the sheet bend can be seen in ancient Egyptian art, but its name first appeared in print in 1794. The sheet was originally the rope attached to the clew, the lower corner of a sail, which was used for trimming a sail. Traditionally, this knot also joins the two corners of a flag to the rope used for raising and lowering it.

Make a bight in the end of one of the ropes to be tied.

2 Take the second rope and tuck its end up through the bight in the first rope.

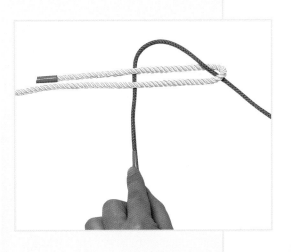

3 Pass the working end of the second rope under the bight in the first rope.

4 Tuck the working end under itself, making sure that both short ends are situated on the same side of the completed knot.

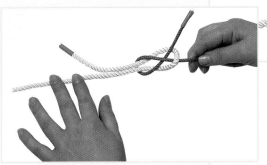

Tighten the knot by pulling on the standing part of the second rope. Trim the working ends if desired.

One-way sheet bend

Dragging a sheet bend over, or through, any obstruction, like a rocky crevice, can lead to the knot sticking. The one-way sheet bend produces a more streamlined knot, but do remember that the short ends should point away from the direction in which the knot is being pulled.

Make a bight in the end of one of the ropes to be tied.

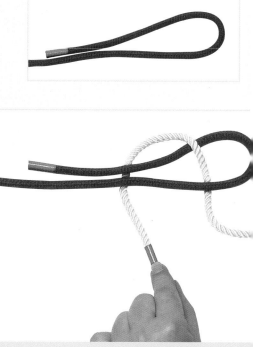

2 Take the second rope and tuck its end up through the bight in the first rope.

3 Pass the working end of the second rope under the bight in the first.

Tuck the working end under itself, making sure that both short ends are situated on the same side of the knot.

5 Bring the working end around and then back on itself to make a figure of eight.

Tuck the working end beneath itself and lay it alongside the two parts of the other rope. Tighten carefully, making sure that all of the knot parts lie snugly together.

175

Racking bend

Where a sheet bend may not be secure enough, try this racking bend. Racking is the name for figure-of-eight interweaving. The temporary racking bend is used particularly when small-diameter messenger lines seize the bight of a much thicker rope, gripping the larger rope so that the bight remains closed.

Make a bight in the larger of the two lines that are to be linked.

Bring the working end of the smaller line over the bight of the larger.

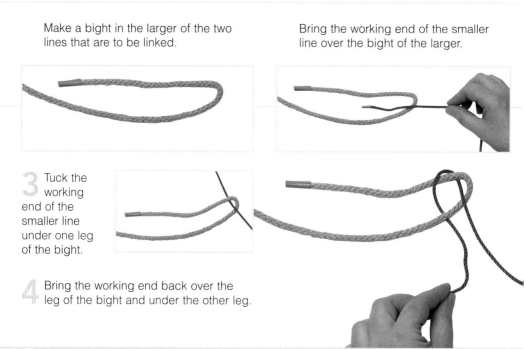

3 Tuck the working end of the smaller line under one leg of the bight.

4 Bring the working end back over the leg of the bight and under the other leg.

Take the working end over the leg of the
bight and under the other leg.

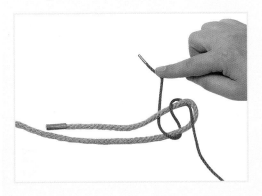

Continue this figure-of-eight racking as
far along the neck of the bight as
needed to keep it together.

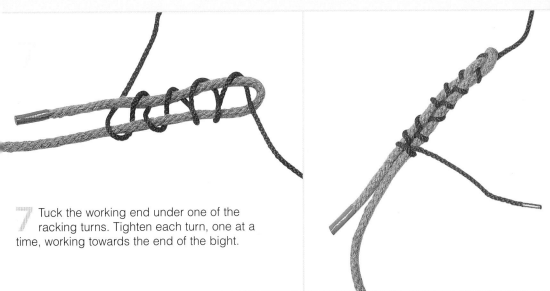

7 Tuck the working end under one of the
racking turns. Tighten each turn, one at a
time, working towards the end of the bight.

Heaving-line bend

First mentioned in 1912 in a Swedish knot manual, De Viktigaste Knutarna, by Hjalmar Ohrvall, this quick and easy knot was used to attach a lightweight messenger line to the bight, or eye, of the heavier hawser that was to be hauled into position.

1 Make a bight in the hawser to be hauled.

Take the lighter line and lay it over the bight so that both working ends are next to each other.

Take the working end of the lighter line around and under the standing part of the bight and then bring it over its own standing part.

Take the working end of the lighter line under the short leg of the bight.

5 Bring the working end of the lighter line back over the two legs of the bight and tuck it underneath itself.

Flemish bend *(also known as figure-of-eight bend)*

A simple knot to tie, this is also one of the strongest bends that you can tie in both rope and string. Mariners, however, aren't that keen on this knot, because it jams in natural cordage. It suits synthetic ropes perfectly though, and is therefore well-liked by climbers.

Make a loop in one end of a length of rope so that the working end lies on top of the standing part.

Hold the loop and give it a half-twist.

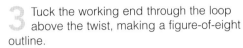

3 Tuck the working end through the loop above the twist, making a figure-of-eight outline.

4 Pick up the working end of the second length of rope and place it parallel to the first working end.

5 Follow the lead of the first rope with the working end of the second rope, keeping to the outside of the first bend.

6 Continue to follow the lead around and transfer to the inside of the second bend. Tighten the knot by pulling on each working end and standing part in turn.

Zeppelin bend

As the name suggests, this bend was used to moor dirigibles (Zeppelins) to the ground or to landing masts. Try it out for yourself on kites.

1 Hold the two ropes together, with their working ends in the same direction.

Taking the rope nearest to you, make a loop in the working end.

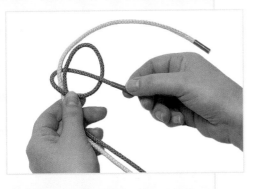

3 Take the working end behind both ropes and bring it back through its own loop.

4 Lift the standing part of the other length of rope towards its working end, so that it lies over its working end.

Pass the working end of the second piece of rope beneath its own standing part and tuck it through the loop now formed and that in the first rope.

Pull on both working ends and standing parts to remove any slack and tighten the knot.

183

Fisherman's knot

(also known as angler's knot, Englishman's bend and halibut knot)

This is a simple, yet effective, knot, and one of the commonest knots used by anglers. Used to tie together two ropes or lines of small and equal diameter, it is formed from two overhand knots that are pushed together so that the short working ends lie in opposite directions. If it is made in rope or cord it can be untied; if it is made in string, you'll have to cut off the knot.

Lay the two lines parallel and close to one another, with the working ends of each facing in opposite directions.

Pick up the lower working end and tie an overhand knot around the upper line.

3 Take the upper working end and tie an overhand knot around the lower line.

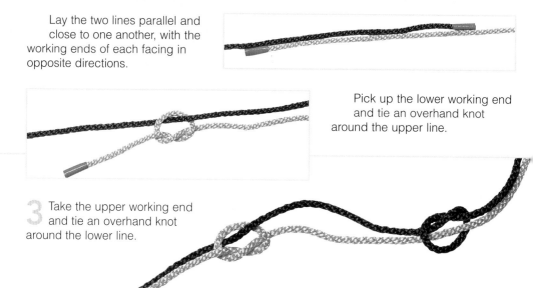

Tighten the individual knots by pulling on both working ends.

5 To unite the knots and tighten them, pull on the standing parts.

TIP: Prevent the short ends of the knot from working loose by taping the working ends to the standing parts with adhesive tape.

Simple Simon over

This knot was devised by knot-tyer extraordinaire Harry Asher, and was first published as recently as 1989. A very useful knot for tying in slippery line, Asher also devised a variation, the Simple Simon under.

In one of the two lines to be joined, make a bight.

Bring the working end of the second line over the bight in the first.

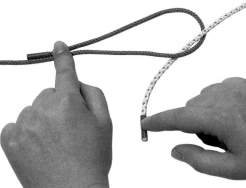

3 Tuck the working end of the second line down through the bight.

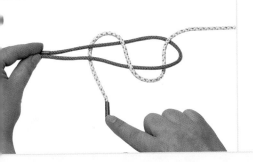

4 Forming a snaking 'S' track, take the working end over, and then behind, the two legs of the bight.

Lay the working end over its preceding part. (This gives the 'over' part of the knot's name. For the Simple Simon under, take the working end under its preceding part.)

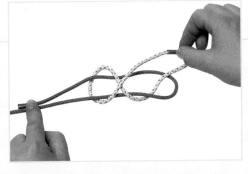

Take the working end around the outside of the bight, and then through the bight, so that it finally lies alongside its own standing part. Gradually work out the slack and tighten the knot.

Double figure-of-eight bend

Both faces of this knot are of the same appearance; compare it to the fisherman's knot, which has one face identical to the double figure-of-eight. Leaving the knots a couple of inches apart on the double figure-of eight will produce a knot that will absorb a sudden shock or jerk by sliding before it holds.

1 Make a loop in one end of a length of rope so that the working end lies on top of the standing part.

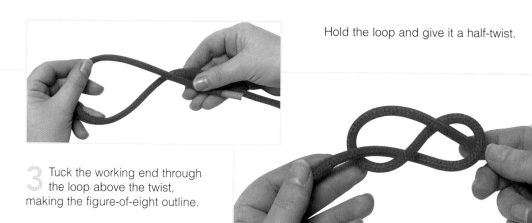

Hold the loop and give it a half-twist.

3 Tuck the working end through the loop above the twist, making the figure-of-eight outline.

4 Insert the working end of the second length of rope through the first knot.

Pull on one working end and its adjacent standing part, then pull on the other working end and its adjacent standing part.

Pull on the working ends to remove any slack from the individual knots.

7 To bring the two knots together, pull on both standing parts.

Adjustable bend

Like the double figure-of-eight bend, if a sudden shock or extra load is exerted on adjustable-bend knots, they will slide and absorb some of the strain. Under a steady load, however, the knots will remain separate. This knot can be tied in rope, although climbers prefer it in webbing.

Lay the two lengths of cord parallel to each other, with their working ends facing in opposite directions.

Take the working end of the upper cord and make a turn around the other cord, wrapping it towards the nearest end.

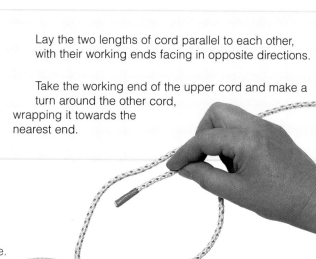

3 Now take the working end around the cord a second time.

Tie a second half-knot, this time right over left.

Bring the working end back down in front of the second line and tuck it under its own final turn.

Turn the half-made knot end-for-end.

Using the second line, make an identical knot approximately 5cm (2 inches) from the first.

Strop bend

This is the knot that schoolgirls usually use to fasten together rubber bands for 'French skipping', but loops of any material, and any colour, can be interlaced in this way.

Bring together two bights and insert one upwards through the other.

Double the working bight of the two back on itself.

3 Pick up the standing parts of the working loop and pull them up and through the secondary loop.

Pull on the two bights in opposite directions.

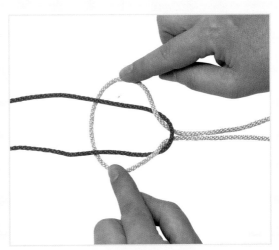

Continue pulling until they are interlocked.

6 Tighten by pulling on both pairs of loop legs at the same time.

Shake hands

A great name for a terrific knot that is not only secure, but also easily untied.

1 In one of the ropes to be joined, make a loop so that the working end lies over the standing part.

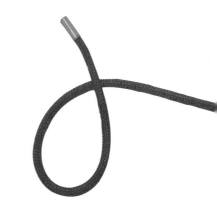

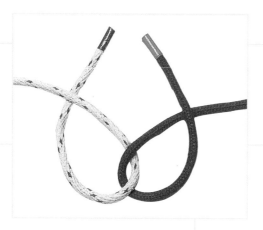

Pass the working end of the second rope up through the first loop and make a second loop with the working end lying under the standing part.

3 Take the first working end and pass it down behind both loops.

Bring the first working end up through the middle (common to both) eye between both loops.

5 Take the second working end and tuck it down through the common central eye, between both loops.

6 Pull on the working ends.

7 Pull on the standing parts to tighten the knot.

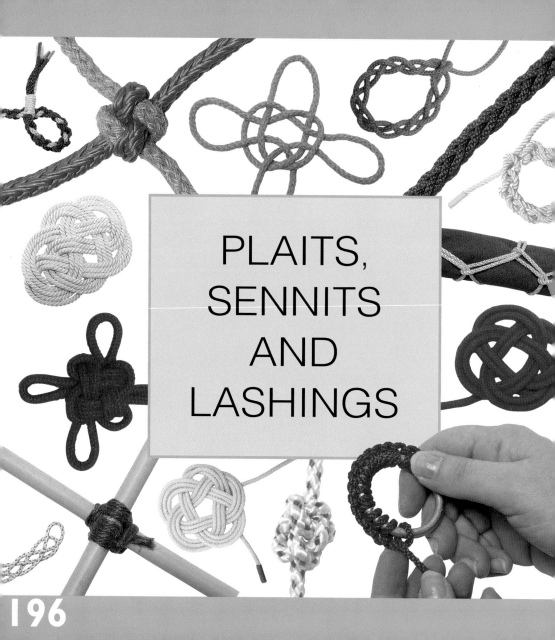

PLAITS, SENNITS AND LASHINGS

A plait is made up of a number of strands of rope interwoven in a simple, repeating pattern, while a sennit is created by a more complex pattern. Both create decorative knots, as well as strong lengths of rope. Lashing is used most often to bind together poles. Also included in this section are a few knots that are so attractive that you'll want to use them for their appearance alone.

Square knot

This knot is also known by a variety of names: rustler's knot, Chinese good-luck knot and Japanese-crown knot are just three. Try it on curtain tie-backs or for dressing-gown belts. This knot works well using two different-coloured cords, as well as flat strips of leather.

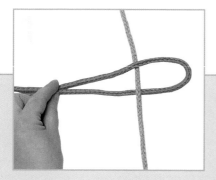

1 Make a bight in the end of one of the cords and pass it over the end of the other cord.

2 Take the working end of the second cord up behind the bight in the first cord.

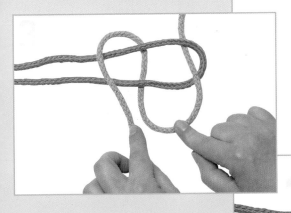

3 Bring the working end of the second cord down over, and in front of, the bight in the first cord.

4 Take the working end of the first cord over the front of the second cord and make a locking tuck through the bight.

5 Flatten and tighten the knot by pulling little by little on each of the four strands in turn.

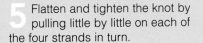

Good-luck knot

When I bought my first car, the previous owner had hung the ignition keys from a short cord tied with this knot. I now use it on gift-wrapped wedding presents for friends; it looks effective, but is easy to tie. For your first attempts, you may like to use some pins to hold the bights in place.

1 Middle a length of cord and make a narrow bight.

2 Keep one finger at the bottom of the bight and pull out a second bight, the same size as the first, in the left-hand leg of the cord.

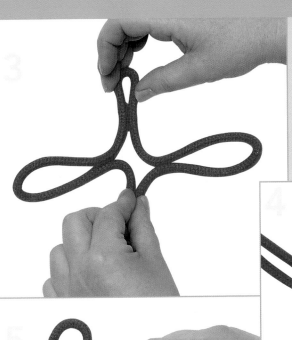

3 Make a third bight the same size, in the right-hand leg of the cord.

4 Lay both of the standing parts of the cord over the left-hand bight.

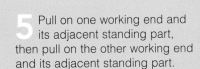

5 Pull on one working end and its adjacent standing part, then pull on the other working end and its adjacent standing part.

6 Pick up the end of the upper bight and lay it over both of the bights that are lying on the right-hand side.

7 Pick up the lower, right-hand bight, take it over the bight that is pointing downwards and then tuck it through beneath the two standing parts of the cord.

8 Carefully tighten the four-part crown without distorting its shape.

9 Bring the left-hand bight diagonally down over the lower bight and then bring the lower bight over it.

10 Bring the right-hand bight over what is now the upper bight.

11 Lead the two strands of the standing parts over the left-hand bight and then tuck it under the two strands of the bent-over lower bight.

12 Tighten the second crown knot.

Chinese lanyard knot

You'll see this very attractive knot tied in coloured silk or cotton cord on Chinese lanterns. It has an unusual, square shape, and although it looks complex, it is, in fact, quite easy to tie - it takes longer to describe it than to tie it! You could use some pins and a piece of polystyrene board to help to keep all of the parts in place while you practice it.

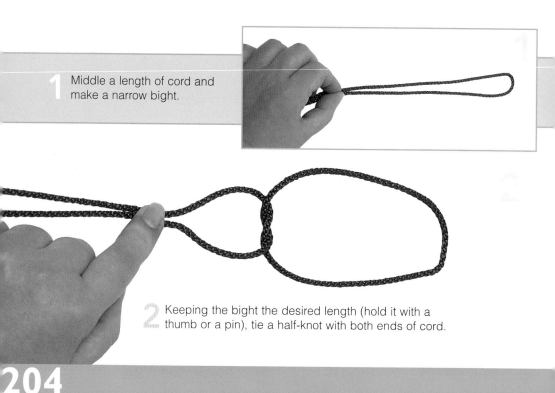

1 Middle a length of cord and make a narrow bight.

2 Keeping the bight the desired length (hold it with a thumb or a pin), tie a half-knot with both ends of cord.

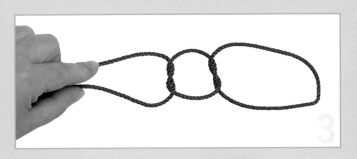

3 Tie a second, identical half-knot with the two ends to complete a loose, open granny knot.

4 Leave a gap of around 7.5cm (3 inches) and tie a second, identical granny knot.

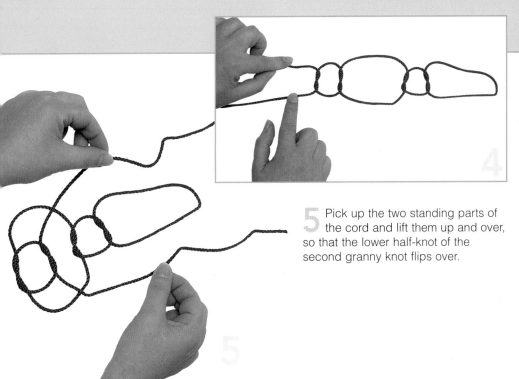

5 Pick up the two standing parts of the cord and lift them up and over, so that the lower half-knot of the second granny knot flips over.

6 Pick up the original bight at the top of the knot and lift it up and forwards so that the upper half-knot of the first granny knot flips over. (The original bight is now lying over all of the knot parts and is pointing downwards.)

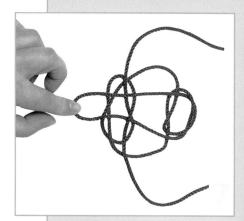

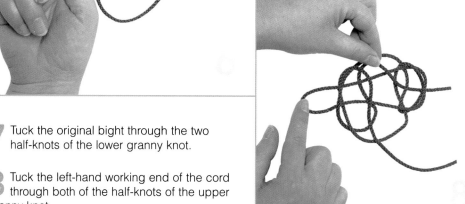

7 Tuck the original bight through the two half-knots of the lower granny knot.

8 Tuck the left-hand working end of the cord through both of the half-knots of the upper granny knot.

9 Carefully lift up the entire knot and turn it over. Pull the new left-hand working end through to the front.

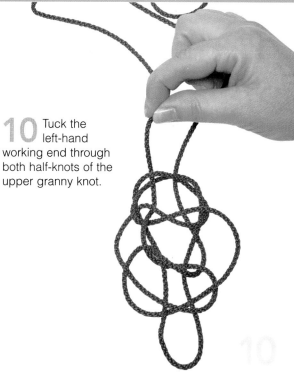

10 Tuck the left-hand working end through both half-knots of the upper granny knot.

11 Make sure that the loop of the bight is long enough to go over the object it will hold, and then slowly, carefully – and patiently – remove the slack by working towards the two working ends.

Chinese button knot

A student from Hong Kong studying fashion design in England showed me how to tie this knot that she used in her collection of 'East-meets-West' clothing. They don't break like ordinary buttons, and they're ideal for pyjamas and underwear because they're soft and don't press into the body. It's an impressive knot, but quite easy to tie, as it is worked flat until it is tightened, and then it becomes round.

1 Middle a length of cord and make an overhand loop so that the working end lies on top of the standing part.

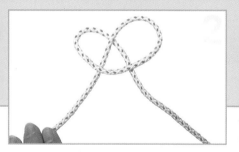

2 Pass the working end down behind the loop that has just been formed to make a 'pretzel' layout.

3 Pick up the other end of the cord and tuck it under, over, under, over. Keep a tight hold at this stage, as the knot will fall apart if you let go.

4 Lead this working end up through the left-hand part of the knot and down through the adjacent eye.

5 Bring the two standing parts together as if you were making a flower stem. Hold the knot flat in the palm of your hand as though it was the head of a flower.

6 Slowly remove the slack from the knot until the knot in your palm becomes convex in shape.

7 Locate the central knot part and carefully prise it back up to the surface.

Jury mast knot *(also known as pitcher knot)*

This flat knot was originally used to rig a makeshift (jury) mast in a boat. It is also said that cannon balls were carried in this knot. Tied in coloured cord, with the working ends led around the edges, such knots could be stitched to scatter cushions for a decorative effect.

1 Pass the rope behind itself to make three large, loose, crossing turns, with each turn overlapping the previous one.

2 Further overlap the left- and right-hand loops – the right over the left – inside the middle loop.

3 Locate the two strands of the middle loop and take the left-hand strand of the middle loop to the left, going under, then over, the two adjacent strands, to make a long, left-hand loop.

4 Take the right-hand strand of the middle loop to the right, going over, then under, the two adjacent strands, to make a long, right-hand loop.

5 Locate the upper edge of the centre loop and carefully pull it up to make a third, upper loop. Adjust the three loops to form a symmetrical knot.

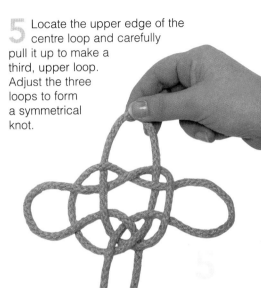

Round mat

This is another 'flat' knot that can be glued or stitched to another surface. It can also be used to place hot pans on.

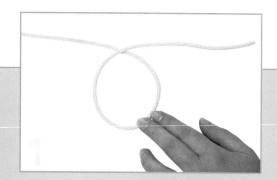

1 Middle a length of cord and make an anti-clockwise overhand loop in the working end.

2 Bring the working end down over the loop and arrange in the 'pretzel' layout.

3 Pick up the other end of the cord and thread it diagonally up and to the left, going over, under, then over, the knot parts.

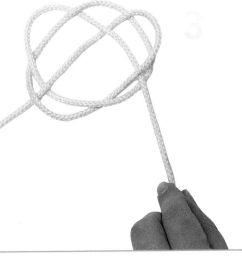

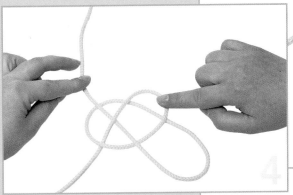

4 Lead the end around clockwise and thread it diagonally to the right, going under, over, under and over.

5 Take the end alongside the standing part and follow the original lead around again to double the knot. (You can make a third turn if you like.) Fix the end in place with glue or a stitch on the underside of the mat.

Carrick mat

Here is another flat mat. Try making it in gold-coloured cord for a decorative effect.

1   In a length of cord, make an overhand loop.

2   Bring the working end down over the loop and make a 'pretzel' layout.

3 Take the working end around from right to left, behind the standing part.

4 Working in a clockwise direction, thread the working end around and through the knot, going over, then under, then over and then under.

5 Tuck the working end alongside and parallel to the standing part and follow the original lead around once (or twice) again to double (or triple) the knot.

215

Ocean plait

You'll need a fairly long length of rope or cord for this mat, and it does help to pin the rope into place until the final locking tuck is made. Some people make these into tablemats, others into doormats, while still others think that they're too good to walk on and hang them on the wall!

1 In one end of a fairly long length of line, make an anti-clockwise overhand loop.

2 Bend the long working end around to the left and lay it over the standing end of the original loop.

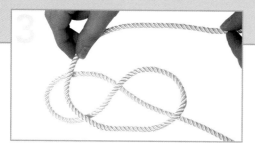

3 Take up the end and lay it from left to right over the top loop.

4 Lead the working end diagonally downwards, from right to left, and lay it on top of the lower loop.

5 Pick up the other half of the line – this is now your new working end – and lay it from left to right over the new standing part.

6 Take the working end diagonally up and to the right, going under, then under again, the nearest loop.

7 Take the working end diagonally from right to left, over, then under, then over and then under, the knot parts.

8 Take the working end diagonally from left to right, over, under, over, under and over the knot parts, so that it emerges at the bottom right of the mat.

9 Tuck the working end up alongside, and parallel to, the standing part and follow the lead around once (or twice) more to double (or triple) the knot.

Half-hitching

Secure a long parcel, or even a roll of carpet, with a series of half-hitches at regular intervals.

1 In the end of the line, make a small, fixed loop. Tuck the long end of the line through the small loop to make a sliding loop and slip it over the end of the item to be bound.

2 Make an underhand loop and tie it in the bight.

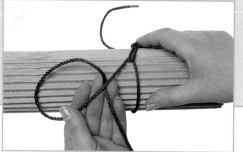

3 Slip this new loop over the end of the item being bound and pull the resulting half-hitch tight.

4 At equal distances along the object being bound, add a series of half-hitches in the same manner.

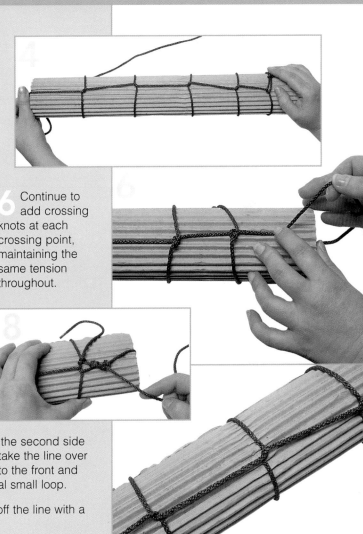

5 When the end of the object is reached, turn it over and, at the first crossing point, tie a crossing knot.

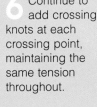

6 Continue to add crossing knots at each crossing point, maintaining the same tension throughout.

7 When you reach the end of the second side of the object being bound, take the line over the end of the object and back to the front and then thread it through the original small loop.

8 Secure the object by tying-off the line with a couple of half-hitches.

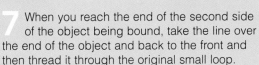

Chain-stitch lashing

Although this lashing uses more line than other forms of lashing, it is very decorative and can be used for gift-wrapping or tying table linen for dinner parties. More usually, it is a good way of securing long, lumpy parcels. It can also be easily undone, simply by pulling on the working end.

1 Tie a small, fixed loop in one end of the line and then pull a bight from the standing part of the line through the loop.

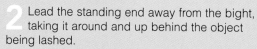

2 Lead the standing end away from the bight, taking it around and up behind the object being lashed.

3 Pull down a second bight from the standing part through the first bight made.

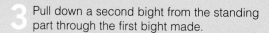

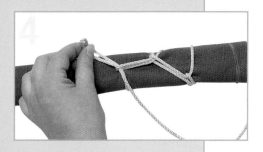

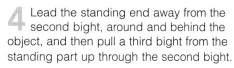
Lead the standing end away from the second bight, around and behind the object, and then pull a third bight from the standing part up through the second bight.

5 Continue with interlacing bights until you reach the end of the object and then pull the working end all the way through the final bight.

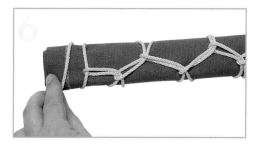

6 Take the working end once around the object and then tuck it under itself.

7 Tuck the working end under its standing part two or three times to secure it.

Square lashing

Square lashing is used to hold two poles at right angles to each other. Use it around the garden to tie up trellises and arbours, or perhaps to make a strong, rustic ladder for a low-level tree house.

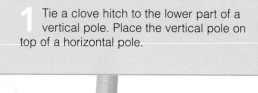

1 Tie a clove hitch to the lower part of a vertical pole. Place the vertical pole on top of a horizontal pole.

2 Wind the rope alternately behind, and then in front of, the upright pole.

3 Pull on the rope to tighten it around the poles; the clove hitch will now slide to one side of the vertical pole.

4 Take the rope over the lower part of the vertical pole, then under the horizontal pole and pull tight on the rope.

5 Complete three more lashing turns around the poles, pulling each one as tight as possible.

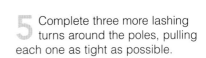

6 Tighten the lashing with a frapping turn by bringing the rope down over the front of the horizontal pole and behind the lower part of the vertical pole. Pull tightly once more.

7 Complete the frapping turn by taking the rope up over the horizontal pole and behind the upper part of the vertical pole and pulling it tight.

8 Make three full frapping turns around the poles.

9   Tie a half-hitch, taking the rope behind and around the lower part of the vertical pole and then tucking it under itself. Pull tight.

10   Tie a second half-hitch to form a clove hitch around the lower part of the vertical pole and pull tight. Trim off any excess rope, but leave a longish end that can be tucked under the lashing.

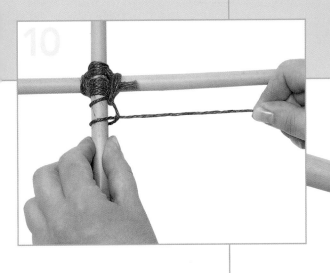

225

Continuous Ring-hitching

This gives a continuous, skinny 'spine' on the outer edge of a narrow ring.

1 Tie two identical half-hitches in a cord.

2 Add a third half-hitch, wrapping and tucking the working end in the same direction as the previous pair of hitches.

3 Continue adding half-hitches, straightening out the work at intervals to make sure that the spine does not twist around the ring.

4 When the working end finally meets up with the standing part, you could try plaiting the two parts together.

Simple chain

This simple chain will shorten a rope
or cord by one-third of its length.

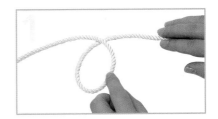

1 Make an anti-clockwise overhand loop with
a long working end.

2 Lay the working end under the loop and pull
through a bight from back to front. Pull the
knot tight.

3 Make a second bight in the working
end and pull it through the first
bight. Now pull it tight.

4 Continue to pull through successive
bights tightening at each stage.

5 To complete the chain, pull the working
end through the final bight completely.

Braid knot

This single-stranded knot replicates a three-stranded pigtail plait. It can be used to shorten a line, to decorate it or to make a thicker handle that won't cut into the hand like a single strand.

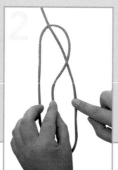

1 Make a long, clockwise underhand loop and then lay all three ropes parallel to each other.

2 Begin to braid the ropes by bringing the right-hand strand over the middle strand to lie inside, and alongside, the left-hand strand.

3 Take the left-hand strand over the middle strand to lie inside, and alongside, the right-hand strand.

4 Repeat steps 2 and 3. (Notice how it is always the outside strand that does all of the work!)

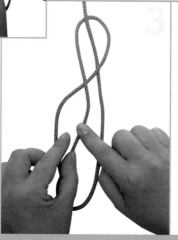

5 Continue to plait alternate right- and left-hand strands, pulling each tightly as you go.

6 At the bottom end of the plait you will notice how a mirror image has accumulated. Untangle this by pulling out the single long working end.

7 Tighten the plait so that a final loop remains at the end.

8 Tuck the working end through the loop to secure the plait.

Four-strand braid

This makes a flat lashing. In stiff stuff it makes an open decorative network or it could be made in decorative cord and stitched to a second surface as a border.

1 Middle two lengths of rope and loop one through the other. Separate the four strands into a right-hand and a left-hand pair.

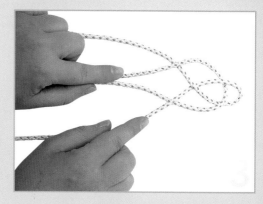

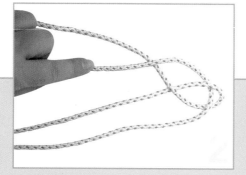

2 Cross the left-hand strand of the left-hand pair over its right-hand strand, going left over right.

3 Cross the left-hand strand of the right-hand pair over the right-hand strand, also going left over right.

4 Cross the innermost strands right over left.

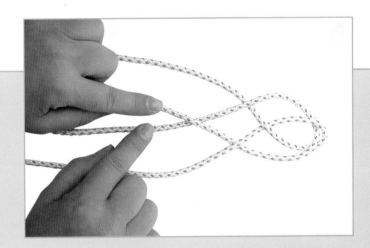

5 Repeat steps 2, 3 and 4, maintaining the tension and tightness throughout to allow the symmetrical pattern to develop. Continue crossing over the strands until the required length is achieved and then bind the ends together.

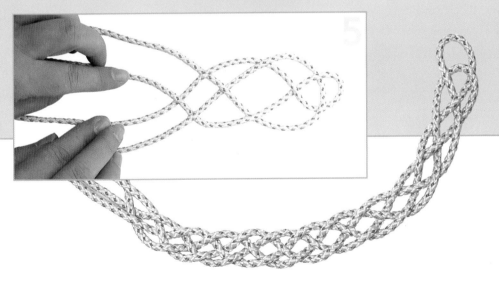

Four-strand sennit

The strength of thin cord or line can be increased fourfold by this plait. It's also an attractive pattern that could be used to make a new lead for a small dog.

1 Bind four strands of rope or cord together and divide them into a left-hand and a right-hand pair.

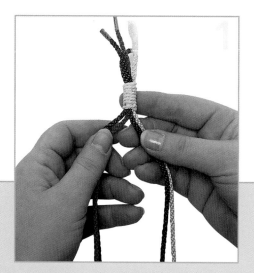

2 Take the outer strand of the right-hand pair behind the other strands and bring it up between the two left-hand strands and back to lie inside, next to its original companion.

3 Take the outer strand of the right-hand pair behind the other strands to emerge between the two left-hand strands and then over, to lie next to its original companion.

4 Repeat steps 2 and 3, keeping an even tension as the work progresses.

5 Continue the process until the required length is achieved and then bind the ends together.

Eight-strand square plait

This is an attractive, herringbone weave that's easier to make than it looks. Try making it using two or more colours.

1 Bind eight strands together and subdivide them into a left-hand and a right-hand group of four.

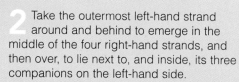

2 Take the outermost left-hand strand around and behind to emerge in the middle of the four right-hand strands, and then over, to lie next to, and inside, its three companions on the left-hand side.

3 Likewise, take the outermost right-hand strand around and behind to emerge in the middle of the four left-hand strands, and then over, to lie next to, and inside, its three companions on the right-hand side.

4 Repeat step 2.

5 Repeat step 3.

6 Continue this process, always using the outermost strands, and tightening as each step is completed. Bind the ends together when the desired length is achieved.

Glossary

ARAMIDES
Synthetic (man-made) fibres.
These fibres do not melt when
heated and their cost limits them
to specialised usage

BEND
The name given to knots that bind
(bend) two separate ropes
together

BIGHT
The slack part of rope between the
two ends that is folded back on
itself to form a narrow loop

BLOOD KNOT
A type of knot secured by
numerous wrapping turns

BODY
The bulky, tied part of a knot

BOLLARD
A small post of wood or metal on a
boat or quay used for securing a
mooring rope

BRAID
Strands of rope plaited or braided
together in a regular pattern.
Generally, a braid is flat or two-
dimensional

BREAKING STRENGTH
The amount of load a new rope
will bear before it breaks. Breaking
strength is reduced by wear and
tear, shock loading and by knots

CABLE
A large rope made by twisting
together three lengths of three-
strand rope

CAPSIZE
What happens when a knot layout
is distorted due to overloading or
overtightening. It may also be
done deliberately as a quick
release mechanism

COIL
Rope wound into neat circles or
loops for storage

CORD
Small stuff under $5/12$in (10mm) in
diameter

CORDAGE
The collective term for ropes of all
sizes and types

CORE
The inner part of a rope made
from parallel, twisted or braided
fibres

CROSSING TURN
A circle made by crossing the
rope over itself

DOUBLE
Used as a verb: to double a knot.
To follow the lead of a knot around
again

ELBOW
Two crossing points made by an
extra twist in a loop

EYE
1) a hole in a knot
2) the hole inside a circle of rope

FIBRE
The smallest element in rope and
cordage

FID
A pointed, wooden tool used for
separating strands of rope

FRAPPING TURNS
Additional turns made across
lashing or whipping turns, used to
tighten the previous layers of turns

FRAY
The deliberate or accidental unlaying
of a rope's end to its components
strands, yarns and fibres

HALF HITCH
A circle of rope made around an object. The circle is kept in place by taking one end of the rope across and at right angles to the other end

HARD LAID
Stiff cordage

HAWSER
Three strand rope

HEAVING LINE
The line attached to a mooring rope. It is thrown from a boat and used to haul the mooring rope to shore

HITCH
A knot used to make a line fast to an anchor point such as a rail, post, ring or other rope

KARIBINER
A metal snap-ring, often D-Shaped, with a pivoting gate that can be closed securely. They are used by climbers and cavers

KERNMANTLE
Climbing rope constructed from a core (kern) of parallel bunches of fibres contained within a tightly woven protective sheath (mantel)

KNOT
1) the term for stoppers, loops and self-sufficient bindings (thereby excluding hitches and bends)
2) the generic term for the tucks and ties made in cordage

LAID ROPE
Rope formed by twisting strands of yarn together

LASH/LASHING
To secure two or more adjacent or crossed poles with a binding of rope

LASHING TURN
The turn used to bind poles together

LANYARD
A short length of cord that is used to lash, secure or suspend an object

LAY
The direction in which rope strands spiral as they go away from the viewer, either clockwise (right-handed or Z laid) or anti-clockwise (left-handed or S laid)

LEAD (pronounced 'leed')
The direction taken by the working end as it goes around or through an object or knot

LINE
Any rope with a specific function, eg.washing line, a tow line

LOCKING TUCK
The finishing lead of a working end that secures the knot in its finished form and without which the knot would unravel

LOOP
A circle of rope formed by bringing two parts of rope together but without them crossing over each other

MARLINESPIKE
A slim, pointed, metal cone used to separate strands of rope, usually when untying a knot

MESSENGER
The name given to a heaving or throwing line when it is used to haul or pull a thicker rope across an intervening space

MIDDLE
To middle: to find the centre of a length of rope by bringing the two ends together

NATURAL FIBRES
Plant products used to make ropes and other cordage

NOOSE
A loop which passes around its own standing part and draws tight when pulled

OVERHAND LOOP
A loop in which the working end is laid on top of the standing part

PALM
A glove-like leather strap with a metal plate (iron) in the palm used to protect the hand when pushing a sailmaker's needle through rope

PRUSIKING
To climb a rope using knots that jam when downwards pressure is applied but can slide up the rope when the weight is removed

RACKING TURNS
Seizing and lashing turns made in a figure-of-eight fashion

ROPE
Cordage over $5/12$in (10mm) in diameter

ROUND TURN
A complete circle followed by a half circle with part of a rope around an object

S-LAID
Left-handed or anticlockwise laid rope

SHOCK CORD
Rope with a very high degree of elasticity. (Also called elasticated cord)

SEIZING
Joining two ropes or parts of ropes together by binding with twine

SLING
An endless rope or webbing 'strop' (pronounced 'strap')

SMALL STUFF
A general, albeit imprecise, term for small diameter 'stuff' like string which is not rope!

SOFT LAID
Flexible rope or cordage (as opposed to hard laid)

STANDING END
The 'inactive' end of rope or cord

STANDING PART
The length of rope or cord between the working and standing ends

STRAND
The largest element of a rope, made from twisted yarns

STROP (pronounced 'strap')
A sling

TAPE
Flat, woven webbing used by climbers to make slings/strops

THREE STRAND ROPE
Rope made of three strands twisted together

TUCK
Passing one part of a rope underneath another part

TURN
Passing the rope around an object

UNDERHAND LOOP
A loop in which the working end is laid beneath the standing part

UNLAID ROPE
Rope that has been separated into its component strands

WHIPPING
A binding used to prevent the ends of rope from fraying

WORKING END
The end of the rope used when tying a knot

YARN
The basic elements of rope strands made from either natural fibres or synthetic (man-made) materials

Z-LAID
Right-handed or clockwise laid rope

Index